Romeo and Juliet

Director's Playbook

About This Playbook
Quick Play Summary
Schema of Scenes
Auditions
The Play
Glossary
Producer Tasks
Pre-Production
Stage Management
Scheduling
Customized Scripts

edited by Sasha Newborn

BANDANNA BOOKS • 2012 • SANTA BARBARA

Romeo and Juliet Director's Playbook copyright © 2012
Bandanna Books ISBN 978-0-942208-65-8
packaged with downloadable custom scripts, also
a reading text *Romeo and Juliet* ISBN 978-0-942208-66-5

CONTENTS

About This Playbook

This book is designed for prospective *directors*, more than half of the pages are for you to fill in with your vision of the play, down to the details of place, date, budget, specific actors, program, etc.

Playbook Package: (free with this book) Downloads for printable scripts for all major roles is at:
shakespeareplaybook.com/romeoscripts/

Reading copies for classroom, text and glossary ($6.95):
https://www.createspace.com/3892597

Director's Tasks

If you've successfully directed plays before, you can skip this section. Otherwise, here are some points to consider:

- A Director knows **how to delegate.** So many details... The first step might be to split responsibilities with a producer or assistant director.
- A Director is willing to make **hard choices,** such as when assigning major roles.
- A Director **inspires confidence.** Being fair but businesslike is a start. Creating a team that can work together, so that all feel a sense of accomplishment—ideal. Demand hard work and reward people when it pays off.
- A Director's overall **vision of the play** helps others understand how they fit in. Shakespeare directors often experiment with setting the play in a specific era (or the future), perhaps to make a point of comparison to current events, such as bullying, or a recent Appalachian-style feud. Or it could be simply a great vehicle for aspiring actors. Whatever it is, strive to share your conception with the costumer, set designer, actors, so they may participate in, and perhaps improve on, that shared vision.
- A Director is a coach, an administrator, a front person, fundraiser, organizer, boss, den mother, and is invested in every person backstage or onstage. Good luck.

As for the book itself, a large swath of blank paper has been reserved for you in every part of every scene of the script. Make this *your* playbook. Fill it with sketches, notes, costume design, sets, scenery, props, expressions, actions—ideas good and bad, just as Orson Welles or Alfred Hitchcock did in preparing for a production. That's the fun part. Scenes will have a blank stage diagram for sketching in sets.

Certain decisions must be considered before production can begin. Is there enough money or the prospect of getting the funds necessary—and on the other side, how much will it cost? Will all the actors be volunteers? The crew? The equipment, costumes, sets, props? How much time is required before opening night? You'll find those nuts and bolts pages to fill in, in the back section, along with some suggestions for creating a program, promotion, and such.

Once the big decision—**to go ahead**—has been made, however, the "directorial" part of being a director comes into play.

- **The arc.** What's this play about? That's the reason for this playbook—as you start to fill in your conception of the play, act by act, you will also begin unconsciously characterizing the roles—how immature are Juliet and Romeo? Do we see their characters emerge before they meet? Do they change/grow over time? Are there clues about the origin of the family animosities?

- **Audition:** As you begin to *see* these characters in your mind, you can start filling in the Audition section—so many to choose among. Many of the characters can be defined by family relationships. So when it comes to actual auditions, you know what to look for: talent and a good fit. Amateur actors may need coaching, or simply encouragement. Lines, lines, lines—a number of long speeches in this play.

Quick Play Summary

Act One: The play opens with servants and then members of two opposing houses in confrontation with swords drawn. Even the old patriarchs try to join but their wives prevent them. The Prince admonishes both. Romeo is lovesick over Rosaline. Paris presses his suit to marry the too-young Juliet Capulet. Juliet is cool to the idea. Mercutio tries to shake Romeo's obsession with Rosaline. Romeo crashes a Capulet party and, on first seeing Juliet, forgets about Rosaline. He steals a kiss, then learns she is a Capulet. Juliet is intrigued.

Act Two: Romeo goes back to the Capulet estate, overhears Juliet at her balcony. They talk, testing each other's love. Romeo arranges a secret wedding. Mercutio, Benvolio, Romeo exchange witticisms. Friar Laurence weds them in private.

Act Three: Mercutio faces off with Tybalt, Romeo intervenes, but Tybalt kills Mercutio. Romeo kills Tybalt—and is banished by the Prince. Master Capulet schemes to quickly marry Juliet to Paris. Romeo spends his last night in Verona with Juliet.

Act Four: Paris sees Friar Laurence to plan the marriage; meets Juliet there. When Paris leaves, the Friar offers a way out—a 42-hour drug that simulates death. At home, Juliet feigns repentance; then takes the potion. The household is frantic in preparation for a wedding. Nurse finds her cold on the bed, apparently dead. The celebration will be a lamentation.

Act Five: Romeo in Mantua hears of Juliet's "death," procures a deadly poison, and dashes back to Verona Friar Laurence discovers that his letter explaining the ruse to Romeo never arrived, and hurries to the Capulet vault. Paris had already gone there, and Romeo arrives. They fight, Paris is killed, Romeo, seeing Juliet "dead," kills himself. Juliet awakes, sees Romeo dead, and stabs herself to death. Friar Laurence tells the tale. The two old patriarchs reach out to each other.

Entrances and Exits

Contents, with a skeleton summary of actors entering and exiting in each scene. Pages numbers in parentheses are the same pages in the reading copies of *Romeo and Juliet.*

4 *Capulet's house* 150(63)

> Lady Capulet
> Nurse
> Capulet
< Lady Capulet
< Nurse
> two Fellows
< First Fellow
< Second Fellow
> (music heard)
> Nurse
< Capulet
< All

5 *Juliet's chamber* 152(64)

> Juliet (supine on bed)
> Nurse
> Lady Capulet
> Capulet
> Friar Laurence
> Count Paris
> Musicians
< the Capulets, Paris, Friar Laurence
< Nurse
> Peter
< Peter
< Musicians

ACT FIVE

1 *Mantua, a street* 160(68)

> Romeo
> Balthasar
< Balthasar
> Apothecary
< Romeo
< Apothecary

2 *Verona, Friar Laurence's cell* 166(70)

> Friar John
> Friar Laurence
< Friar John
< Friar Laurence

3 *Churchyard, Capulet sepulcher* 168(71)

> Paris
> Page <
< Paris (hiding)
> Romeo
> Balthasar
< Balthasar (away)
> Paris (emerges)
> Page <
< Paris (dies)
< Romeo (dies)
> Friar Laurence
> Balthasar < (stays away)
> Juliet (awakens)
< Friar Laurence
> Chief Watch
< Juliet (dies)
> Page
> Watchmen
< one Watchman
< the other Watchmen
> Balthasar with Watchman
> Friar Laurence with Watchman
> Prince and his party
> Capulet and Lady Capulet
> Montague and Lady Montague and others
< All

Auditions

Advice specific to this play: Great play for character actors as well as the leads. The Nurse, Old Capulet, Mercutio, Friar Laurence all have their scenes. Actors for both Juliet and Romeo need to show broad and deep range, and what one might call volatility. an ability to hold an audience in solo scenes.

Some directors use "cold" readings (unrehearsed) for first auditions. And, if the actor is worth a second call, assign a few pages to rehearse, so that you can hear a more nuanced reading. Even better, pair up two actors to dialogue.

Auditions for the **major roles should be done early** in the process. As you become familiar with these actors, you can better visualize scenes, and thus begin to flesh out the vision of the drama, with your available talent. Equally important, the actors begin to bond among themselves as part of *the cast*.

Prepare **understudies** for the major roles, so that, if the occasion arises, they are prepared to step in at the last minute. Do *you* have an understudy, an assistant director?

Should everyone see everything? No need, but someone must be in charge of scheduling and reminders.

This play has a plethora of extras for crowd scenes, parties, officials—and it shouldn't look like the same crowd. Though they have no lines, they may be noisy and know when and where to position themselves and when to exit.

As director, you have the **prerogative to make changes** in the play as you see fit—from costuming and set design to cutting lines that don't work, sometimes (gasp) cutting whole scenes or characters—anything that makes the play work better.

Romeo, a Montague:

Juliet, a Capulet:

Mercutio:

Benvolio:

Montague:

Lady Montague:

Capulet:

Lady Capulet:

Tybalt:

Friar Laurence:

Friar John:

Balthasar:

Abram:

Sampson:

Gregory:

Escalus, Prince of Verona:

Paris:

Peter:

Apothecary:

Musicians:

Various Citizens, Officials, Servants, and Attendants:

CREW

Assistant director: advisor to director, taking care of details, able to step in if necessary.

Producer: in charge of the business end: budget, ticket office, ushers, money, fundraising (if necessary), publicity, program, theater rental.

Costume Designer: wardrobe for the cast

Set Designer: moveable sets, backdrops, materials

Stage Manager: responsible for who and what goes where and when backstage and onstage, when the curtain falls or opens.

Lighting: lights on stage and in theater

Sound: sound effects, will there be a live band, perhaps the Players?

And each of these functions may have a budget for expenses, or need for volunteers or helpers.

Prologue

1

[*Empty stage*]

Announcer: Two households, both alike in dignity,
In fair Verona, where we lay our scene,
From ancient grudge break to new mutiny,
Where civil blood makes civil hands unclean.
From forth the fatal loins of these two foes
A pair of star-crossed lovers take their life;
Whose misadventured piteous overthrows
Does with their death bury their parents' strife.
The fearful passage of their death-marked love,
And the continuance of their parents' rage,
Which, but their children's end, naught could remove,
Is now the two hours' traffic of our stage;
The which if you with patient ears attend,
What here shall miss, our toil shall strive to mend.

[*Exit*]

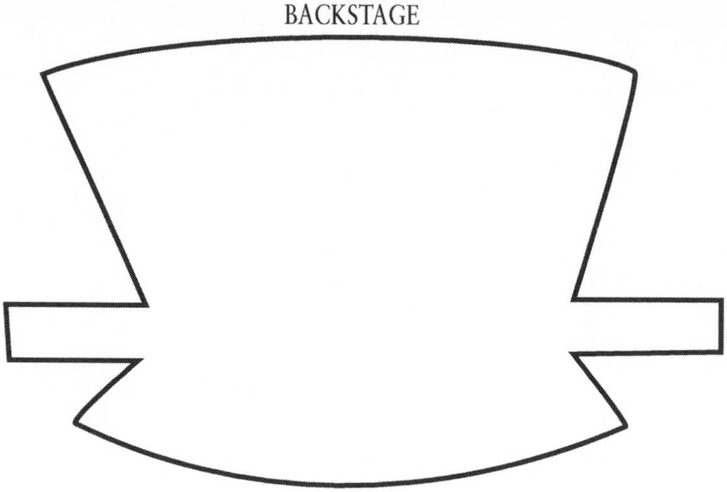

Act One

1

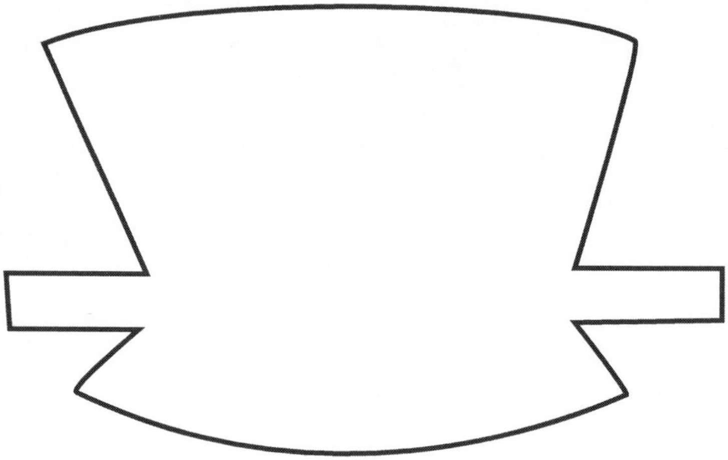

[*A street in Verona*]

[*Enter Sampson and Gregory, Capulet servants*]

Sampson: Gregory, on my word, we'll not carry coals.

Gregory: No, for then we should be colliers.

Sampson: I mean, though we be in choler, we'll draw.

Gregory: Ay, while you live, draw your neck out of collar.

Sampson: I strike quickly, being moved.

Gregory: But you are not quickly moved to strike.

Sampson: A dog of the house of Montague moves me.

Gregory: To move is to stir, and to be valiant is to stand. Therefore, if you are moved, you run away.

Sampson: A dog of that house shall move me to stand. I will take the wall of any man or maid of Montague's.

Gregory: That shows you a weak slave; for the weakest goes to the wall.

Sampson: 'Tis true; and therefore women, being the weaker vessels, are ever thrust to the wall. Therefore I will push Montague's men from the wall and thrust his maids to the wall.

Gregory: The quarrel is between our masters and us their men.

Sampson: 'Tis all one. I will show myself a tyrant. When I have fought with the men, I will be cruel with the maids—I will cut off their heads.

Gregory: The heads of the maids?

Sampson: Ay, the heads of the maids, or their maidenheads. Take it in what sense you will.

Gregory: They must take it in sense that feel it.

Sampson: Me they shall feel while I am able to stand; and 'tis known I am a pretty piece of flesh.

Gregory: 'Tis well you are not fish; if you had, you had been poor-John. Draw your tool! Here comes two of the house of Montagues.

[*Enter Abram and Balthasar*]

Sampson: My naked weapon is out. Quarrel! I will back you.

Gregory: How? turn your back and run?

Sampson: Fear me not.

Gregory: No, indeed. I fear you!

Sampson: Let us take the law of our sides; let them begin.

Gregory: I will frown as I pass by, and let them take it as they list.

Sampson: Nay, as they dare. I will bite my thumb at them; which is disgrace to them, if they bear it.

Abram: Do you bite your thumb at us, sir?

Sampson: I do bite my thumb, sir.

Abram: Do you bite your thumb at us, sir?

Sampson: [*aside to Gregory*] Is the law of our side if I say yes?

Gregory: [*aside to Sampson*] No.

Sampson: No, sir, I do not bite my thumb at you, sir; but I bite my thumb, sir.

Gregory: Do you quarrel, sir?

Abram: Quarrel, sir? No, sir.

Sampson: But if you do, sir, am for you. I serve as good a man as you.

Abram: No better.

Sampson: Well, sir.

[*Enter Benvolio*]

Gregory: [*aside to Sampson*] Say "better." Here comes one of my master's kinsmen.

Sampson: Yes, better, sir.

Abram: You lie.

Sampson: Draw, if you be men. Gregory, remember your swashing blow.

[*They fight*]

Do you bite your thumb at us, sir?

Benvolio: Part, fools! [*Beats down their swords*] Put up your swords. You know not what you do.

[*Enter Tybalt*]

Tybalt: What, are you drawn among these heartless hinds?
Turn you, Benvolio! look upon your death.

Benvolio: I do but keep the peace. Put up your sword,
Or manage it to part these men with me.

Tybalt: What, drawn, and talk of peace? I hate the word
As I hate hell, all Montagues, and you.
Have at you, coward!

[*They fight*]

[*Enter an officer, and several Citizens with clubs*]

Officer: Clubs, bills, and partisans! Strike! beat them down!

Citizens: Down with the Capulets! Down with the Montagues!

[*Enter Old Capulet in his gown, and his Wife*]

Capulet: What noise is this? Give me my long sword, ho!

Lady Capulet: A crutch, a crutch! Why call you for a sword?

Capulet: My sword, I say! Old Montague is come
And flourishes his blade in spite of me.

[*Enter Old Montague and his Wife*]

Montague: You villain Capulet! Hold me not, let me go.

Lady Montague: You shall not stir one foot to seek a foe.

[*Enter Prince Escalus, with his Train*]

Prince: Rebellious subjects, enemies to peace,
Profaners of this neighbor-stained steel—
Will they not hear? What, ho! you men, you beasts,
That quench the fire of your pernicious rage
With purple fountains issuing from your veins!
On pain of torture, from those bloody hands
Throw your mistempered weapons to the ground
And hear the sentence of your moved prince.
Three civil brawls, bred of an airy word
By you, old Capulet, and Montague,
Have thrice disturbed the quiet of our streets
And made Verona's ancient citizens
Cast by their grave beseeming ornaments
To wield old partisans, in hands as old,
Cankered with peace, to part your cankered hate.
If ever you disturb our streets again,
Your lives shall pay the forfeit of the peace.
For this time all the rest depart away.
You, Capulet, shall go along with me;
And, Montague, come you this afternoon,
To know our farther pleasure in this case,
To old Freetown, our common judgment place.
Once more, on pain of death, all men depart.

[*Exit crowd and Prince*]

If ever you disturb our streets again,your lives shall pay the forfeit

Montague: Who set this ancient quarrel new abroach?
Speak, nephew, were you by when it began?

Benvolio: Here were the servants of your adversary
And yours, close fighting before I did approach.
I drew to part them. In the instant came
The fiery Tybalt, with his sword prepared;
Which, as he breathed defiance to my ears,
He swung about his head and cut the winds,
Who, nothing hurt withal, hissed him in scorn.
While we were interchanging thrusts and blows,
Came more and more, and fought on part and part,
Till the Prince came, who parted either part.

Lady Montague: O, where is Romeo? Saw you him today?
Right glad I am he was not at this fray.

Benvolio: Madam, an hour before the worshipped sun
Peered forth the golden window of the East,
A troubled mind drove me to walk abroad;
Where, underneath the grove of sycamore
That westward roots from the city's side,
So early walking did I see your son.
Towards him I made; but he was aware of me
And stole into the covert of the wood.
I—measuring his affections by my own,
Which then most sought where most might not be found,
Being one too many by my weary self—
Pursued my humor, not pursuing his,
And gladly shunned who gladly fled from me.

Montague: Many a morning has he there been seen,
With tears augmenting the fresh morning's dew,
Adding to clouds more clouds with his deep sighs;
But all so soon as the all-cheering sun
Should in the farthest East began to draw
The shady curtains from Aurora's bed,
Away from light steals home my heavy son
And private in his chamber pens himself,
Shuts up his windows, locks fair daylight
And makes himself an artificial night.
Black and portentous must this humor prove
Unless good counsel may the cause remove.

Benvolio: My noble uncle, do you know the cause?

Montague: I neither know it nor can learn of him

Benvolio: Have you importuned him by any means?

Montague: Both by myself and many other friend;
But he, his own affections' counsellor,
Is to himself—I will not say how true—
But to himself so secret and so close,
So far from sounding and discovery,
As is the bud bit with an envious worm
Before he can spread his sweet leaves to the air
Or dedicate his beauty to the sun.
Could we but learn from whence his sorrows grow,
We would as willingly give cure as know.

O, where is Romeo? Saw you him today?

[*Enter Romeo*]

Benvolio: See, where he comes. So please you step aside,
I'll know his grievance, or be much denied.

Montague: I would you were so happy by your stay
To hear true shrift. Come, madam, let's away,

[*Exit Montague and Lady Montague*]

Benvolio: Good morrow, cousin.

Romeo: Is the day so young?

Benvolio: But new struck nine.

Romeo: Ay me! sad hours seem long.
Was that my father that went away so fast?

Benvolio: It was. What sadness lengthens Romeo's hours?

Romeo: Not having that which having makes them short.

Benvolio: In love?

Romeo: Out—

Benvolio: Of love?

Romeo: Out of her favor where I am in love.

Benvolio: Alas that love, so gentle in his view,
Should be so tyrannous and rough in proof!

Romeo: Alas that love, whose view is muffled still,
Should without eyes see pathways to his will!
Where shall we dine? O me! What fray was here?
Yet tell me not, for I have heard it all.
Here's much to do with hate, but more with love.
Why then, O brawling love! O loving hate!
O anything, of nothing first create!
O heavy lightness! serious vanity!
Misshapen chaos of well-seeming forms!
Feather of lead, bright smoke, cold fire, sick health!
Still-waking sleep, that is not what it is
This love feel I, that feel no love in this.
Do you not laugh?

Benvolio: No, cuz, I rather weep.

Romeo: Good heart, at what?

Benvolio: At your good heart's oppression.

Romeo: Why, such is love's transgression.
Griefs of my own lie heavy in my breast,
Which you will propagate, to have it pressed
With more of yours. This love that you have shown
Does add more grief to too much of my own.
Love is a smoke raised with the fume of sighs;
Being purged, a fire sparkling in lovers' eyes;
Being vexed, a sea nourished with lovers' tears.
What is it else? A madness most discreet,
A choking gall, and a preserving sweet.
Farewell, my cuz.

Benvolio: Soft! I will go along.
But if you leave me so, you do me wrong.

Romeo: Tut! I have lost myself; I am not here:
This is not Romeo, he's some other where.

Benvolio: Tell me in sadness, who is that you love?

Romeo: What, shall I groan and tell you?

Benvolio: Groan? Why, no;
But sadly tell me who.

Romeo: Bid a sick man in sadness make his will.
Ah, word ill urged to one that is so ill!
In sadness, cousin, I do love a woman.

Benvolio: I aimed so near when I supposed you loved.

Romeo: A right good markman! And she's fair I love.

Benvolio: A right fair mark, fair cuz, is soonest hit.

Romeo: Well, in that hit you miss. She'll not be hit
With Cupid's arrow. She has Dian's wit,
And, in strong proof of chastity well armed,
From Love's weak childish bow she lives unharmed.
She will not stay the siege of loving terms,
Nor bide the encounter of assailing eyes,
Nor open her lap to saint-seducing gold.
O, she's rich in beauty; only poor
That, when she dies, with beauty dies her store.

Benvolio: Then she has sworn that she will still live chaste?

Romeo: She has, and in that sparing makes huge waste;
For beauty, starved with her severity,
Cuts beauty off from all posterity.
She is too fair, too wise, wisely too fair,
To merit bliss by making me despair.
She has forsworn to love, and in that vow
Do I live dead that live to tell it now.

Benvolio: Be ruled by me: forget to think of her.

Romeo: O, teach me how I should forget to think!

Benvolio: By giving liberty unto your eyes.
Examine other beauties.

Romeo: 'Tis the way
To call hers exquisite in question more.
These happy masks that kiss fair ladies' brows,
Being black puts us in mind they hide the fair.
He that is stricken blind cannot forget
The precious treasure of his eyesight lost.
Show me a mistress that is passing fair,
What does her beauty serve but as a note
Where I may read who passed that passing fair?
Farewell. you can not teach me to forget.

Benvolio: I'll pay that doctrine, or else die in debt.

[*Exit*]

In sadness, cousin, I do love a woman.

2

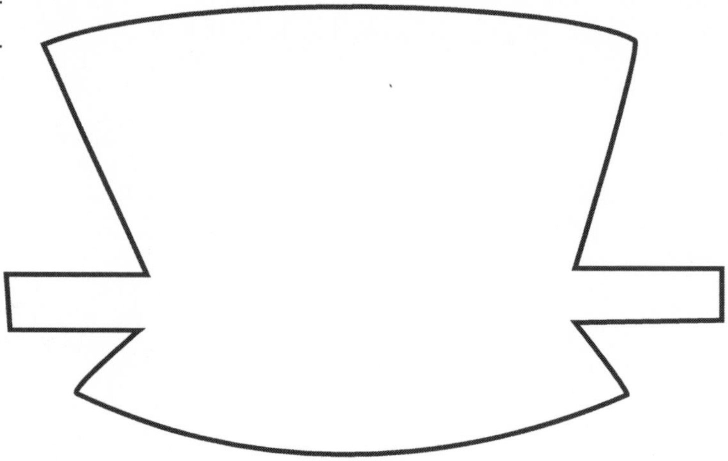

[A Street]

[Enter Capulet, Count Paris, and Servant]

Capulet: But Montague is bound as well as I,
In penalty alike; and 'tis not hard, I think,
For men so old as we to keep the peace.

Paris: Of honorable reckoning are you both,
And pity 'tis you lived at odds so long.
But now, my lord, what say you to my suit?

Capulet: But saying over what I have said before:
My child is yet a stranger in the world,
She has not seen the change of fourteen years;
Let two more summers wither in their pride
Before we may think her ripe to be a bride.

Paris: Younger than she are happy mothers made.

Capulet: And too soon marred are those so early made.
The earth has swallowed all my hopes but she;
She is the hopeful lady of my earth.
But woo her, gentle Paris, get her heart;
My will to her consent is but a part.
If she agree, within her scope of choice
Lies my consent and fair according voice.
This night I hold an old accustomed feast,
Whereto I have invited many a guest,
Such as I love; and you among the store,
One more, most welcome, makes my number more.
At my poor house look to behold this night
Earth-treading stars that make dark heaven light.
Such comfort as do lusty young men feel
When well-apparelled April on the heel
Of limping Winter treads, even such delight
Among fresh female buds shall you this night
Inherit at my house. Hear all, all see,
And like her most whose merit most shall be;
Which, on more view of many, mine, being one,
May stand in number, though in reckoning none.
Come, go with me.

[To Servant, giving him a paper]

Go, sirrah, trudge about
Through fair Verona; find those persons out
Whose names are written there, and to them say,
My house and welcome on their pleasure stay—

[Exit Capulet and Paris]

Servant: Find them out whose names are written here? It is written that the shoemaker should meddle with his yard and the tailor with his last, the fisher with his pencil and the painter with his nets; but I am sent to find those persons whose names are here writ, and can never find what names the writing person has here writ. I must to the learned. In good time!

[*Enter Benvolio and Romeo*]

Benvolio: Tut, man, one fire burns out another's burning;
One pain is lessoned by another's anguish;
Turn giddy, and be holp by backward turning;
One desperate grief cures with another's languish.
Take you some new infection to your eye,
And the rank poison of the old will die.

Romeo: Your plantain leaf is excellent for that.

Benvolio: For what, I pray you?

Romeo: For your broken shin.

Benvolio: Why, Romeo, are you mad?

Romeo: Not mad, but bound more than a madman is;
Shut up in prison, kept without my food,
Whipped and tormented and— Good-day, good fellow.

Servant: G'day. I pray, sir, can you read?

Romeo: Ay, my own fortune in my misery.

Servant: Perhaps you have learned it without book. But I pray, can you read anything you see?

Romeo: Yes, If I know the letters and the language.

Servant: You say honestly. Rest you merry!

Romeo: Stay, fellow; I can read.

[*He reads*]

Signior Martino and his wife and daughters;
Count Anselmo and his beauteous sisters;
The lady widow of Vitruvio;
Signior Placentio and his lovely nieces;
Mercutio and his brother Valentine;
Mine uncle Capulet, his wife, and daughters;
My fair niece Rosaline and Livia;
Signior Valentio and his cousin Tybalt;
Lucio and the lively Helena.

[*Gives back the paper*]

A fair assembly. Where should they come?

Servant: Up.

Romeo: Where?

Servant: To supper, to our house.

Romeo: Whose house?

Servant: My master's.

Romeo: Indeed I should have asked you that before.

Servant: Now I'll tell you without asking. My master is the great rich Capulet; and if you be not of the house of Montagues, I pray come and crush a cup of wine. Rest you merry!

[*Servant Exits*]

G'day. I pray, sir, can you read?

Benvolio: At this same ancient feast of Capulet's
Sups the fair Rosaline whom you so love;
With all the admired beauties of Verona.
Go there, and with unattainted eye
Compare her face with some that I shall show,
And I will make you think your swan a crow.

Romeo: When the devout religion of my eye
Maintains such falsehood, then turn tears to fires;
And these, who, often drowned, could never die,
Transparent heretics, be burnt for liars!
One fairer than my love? The all-seeing sun
Never saw her match since first the world begun.

Benvolio: Tut! you saw her fair, none else being by,
Herself poised with herself in either eye;
But in that crystal scales let there be weighed
Your lady's love against some other maid
That I will show you shining at this feast,
And she shall scant show well that now seems best.

Romeo: I'll go along, no such sight to be shown,
But to rejoice in splendor of my own.

[*Exit*]

3

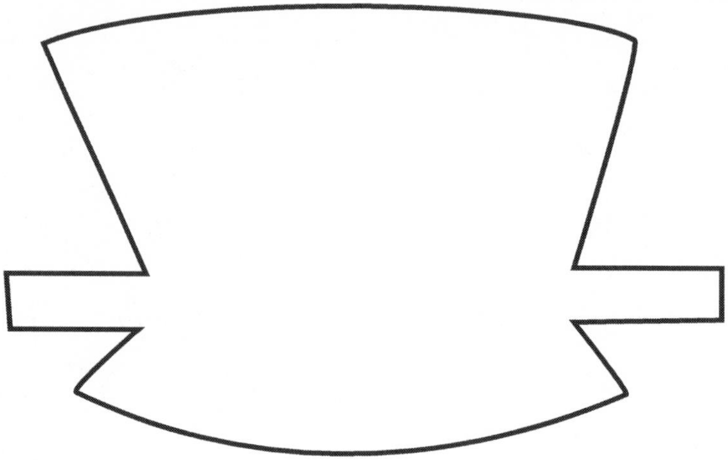

[Capulet's house]

[Enter Capulet's Wife, and Nurse]

Lady Capulet: Nurse, where's my daughter? Call her forth to me.

Nurse: Now, by my maidenhead at twelve year old,
I bade her come. What, lamb! what ladybird!
God forbid! Where's this girl? What, Juliet!

[Enter Juliet]

Juliet: How now? Who calls?

Nurse: Your mother.

Juliet: Madam, I am here.
What is your will?

Lady Capulet: This is the matter— Nurse, give leave awhile,
We must talk in secret. Nurse, come back again;
I have remembered me, you'd hear our counsel.
You know my daughter's of a pretty age.

Nurse: Faith, I can tell her age unto an hour.

Lady Capulet: She's not fourteen.

Nurse: I'll lay fourteen of my teeth—
And yet, to my teeth be it spoken, I have but four—
She is not fourteen. How long is it now
To Lammastide?

Lady Capulet: A fortnight and odd days.

Nurse: Even or odd, of all days in the year,
Come Lammas Eve at night shall she be fourteen.
Susan and she (God rest all Christian souls!)
Were of an age. Well, Susan is with God;
She was too good for me. But, as I said,
On Lammas Eve at night shall she be fourteen;
That shall she, indeed; I remember it well.
'Tis since the earthquake now eleven years;
And she was weaned (I never shall forget it),
Of all the days of the year, upon that day;
For I had then laid wormwood to my dug,
Sitting in the sun under the dovehouse wall.
My lord and you were then at Mantua.
Nay, I do bear a brain. But, as I said,
When it did taste the wormwood on the nipple
Of my dug and felt it bitter, pretty fool,
To see it tetchy and fall out with the dug!
Shake, quotes the dovehouse! 'Twas no need, I trow,
To bid me trudge.
And since that time it is eleven years,
For then she could stand high-alone; nay, by the rood,

She could have run and waddled all about;
For even the day before, she broke her brow;
And then my husband (God be with his soul!
'A was a merry man) took up the child.
"Yea,' quoth he, "Do you fall upon your face?
You will fall backward when you have more wit;
Will you not, Jule?' and, by my holidam,
The pretty wretch left crying, and said "Ay.'
To see now how a jest shall come about!
I warrant, though I should live a thousand yeas,
I never should forget it. "Will you not, Jule?' quoth he,
And, pretty fool, it stinted, and said "Ay.'

Lady Capulet: Enough of this. I pray you hold your peace.

Nurse: Yes, madam. Yet I cannot choose but laugh
To think it should leave crying and say "Ay."
And yet, I warrant, it bad upon it brow
A bump as big as a young cockerel's stone;
A perilous knock; and it cried bitterly.
"Yea," quoth my husband, "fall upon your face?
You will fall backward when you come to age;
Will you not, Jule?" It stinted, and said "Ay."

Juliet: And stint you too, I pray you, nurse, say I.

Nurse: Peace, I have done. God mark you to his grace!
You were the prettiest babe that ever I nursed.
If I might live to see you married once, I have my wish.

Lady Capulet: Marry, that "marry" is the very theme
I came to talk of. Tell me, daughter Juliet,
How stands your disposition to be married?

Juliet: It is an honor that I dream not of.

Nurse: An honor? Were not I your only nurse,
I would say you had sucked wisdom from your teat.

Lady Capulet: Well, think of marriage now. Younger than you,
Here in Verona, ladies of esteem,
Are made already mothers. By my count,
I was your mother much upon these years
That you are now a maid. Thus then in brief:
The valiant Paris seeks you for his love.

Nurse: A man, young lady! Lady, such a man
As all the world— why he's a man of wax.

Lady Capulet: Verona's summer has not such a flower.

Nurse: Nay, he's a flower, in faith— a very flower.

Lady Capulet: What say you? Can you love the gentleman?
This night you shall behold him at our feast.
Read over the volume of young Paris' face,
And find delight writ there with beauty's pen;
Examine every married lineament,
And see how one another lends content;
And what obscured in this fair volume lies
Find written in the margin of his eyes,
This precious book of love, this unbound lover,
To beautify him only lacks a cover.
The fish lives in the sea, and 'tis much pride
For fair without the fair within to hide.
That book in many's eyes does share the glory,
That in gold clasps locks in the golden story;
So shall you share all that he does possess,
By having him making yourself no less.

Nurse: No less? Nay, bigger! Women grow by men.

Lady Capulet: Speak briefly, can you like of Paris' love?

Juliet: I'll look to like, if looking liking move;

The valiant Paris seeks you for his love.

But no more deep will I endart my eye
Than your consent gives strength to make it fly.

[*Enter Servant*]

Servant: Madam, the guests are come, supper served up, you called, my young lady asked for, the nurse cursed in the pantry, and everything in extremity. I must hence to wait. I beseech you follow straight.

Lady Capulet: We follow you.

[*Exit Servant*]

Juliet, the Count stays.

Nurse: Go, girl, seek happy nights to happy days.

[*Exit*]

4

[*A street*]

[*Enter Romeo, Mercutio, Benvolio, Maskers with torches*]

Romeo: What, shall this speech be spoke for our excuse?
Or shall we on without apology?

Benvolio: The date is out of such prolixity.
We'll have no Cupid hoodwinked with a scarf,
Bearing a Tartar's painted bow of lath,
Scaring the ladies like a crowkeeper;
Nor no without book prologue, faintly spoke
After the prompter, for our entrance;
But, let them measure us by what they will,
We'll measure them a measure, and be gone.

Romeo: Give me a torch. I am not for this ambling.
Being but heavy, I will bear the light.

Mercutio: Nay, gentle Romeo, we must have you dance.

Romeo: Not I, believe me. You have dancing shoes
With nimble soles; I have a soul of lead
So stakes me to the ground I cannot move.

Mercutio: You are a lover. Borrow Cupid's wings
And soar with them above a common bound.

Romeo: I am too sore enpierced with his shaft
To soar with his light feathers; and so bound
I cannot bound a pitch above dull woe.
Under love's heavy burden do I sink.

Mercutio: And, to sink in it, should you burden love—
Too great oppression for a tender thing.

Romeo: Is love a tender thing? It is too rough,
Too rude, too boisterous, and it pricks like thorn.

Mercutio: If love be rough with you, be rough with love.
Prick love for pricking, and you beat love down.
Give me a case to put my visage in.
A visor for a visor! What care I
What curious eye does quote deformities?
Here are the beetle brows shall blush for me.

Benvolio: Come, knock and enter; and no sooner in
But every man betake him to his legs.

Romeo: A torch for me! Let wantons light of heart

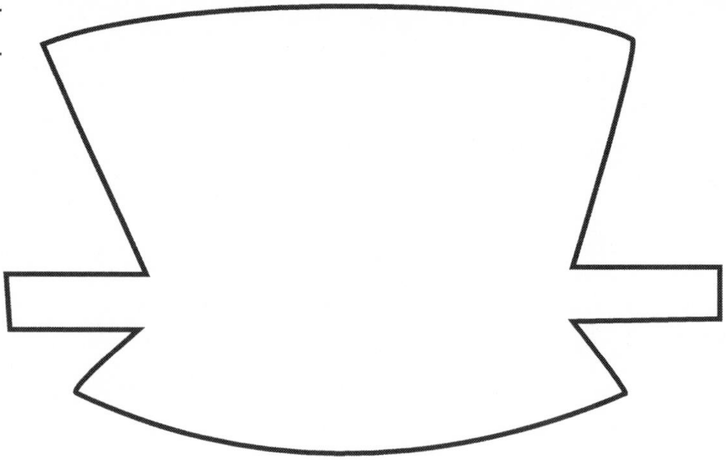

Tickle the senseless rushes with their heels;
For I am proverbed with a grandsire phrase,
I'll be a candle-holder and look on;
The game was never so fair, and I am done.

Mercutio: Tut! dun's the mouse, the constable's own word!
If you are Dun, we'll draw you from the mire
Of this sir-reverence love, wherein you stick
Up to the ears. Come, we burn daylight, ho!

Is love a tender thing? It is too rough,
Too rude, too boisterous

Romeo: Nay, that's not so.

Mercutio: I mean, sir, in delay
We waste our lights in vain, like lamps by day.
Take our good meaning, for our judgment sits
Five times in that before once in our five wits.
Romeo: And we mean well, in going to this masque;
But 'tis no wit to go.

Mercutio: Why, may one ask?

Romeo: I dreamt a dream tonight.

Mercutio: And so did I.

Romeo: Well, what was yours?

Mercutio: That dreamers often lie.

Romeo: In bed asleep, while they do dream things true.

Mercutio: O, then I see Queen Mab has been with you.
She is the fairies' midwife, and she comes
In shape no bigger than an agate stone
On the forefinger of an alderman,
Drawn with a team of little atomies
Athwart men's noses as they lie asleep;
Her wagon spokes made of long spinners' legs,
The cover, of the wings of grasshoppers;
Her traces, of the smallest spider's web;
Her collars, of the moonshine's watery beams;
Her whip, of cricket's bone; the lash, of film;
Her wagoner, a small gray-coated gnat,
Not half so big as a round little worm
Pricked from the lazy finger of a maid;
Her chariot is an empty hazelnut,
Made by the joiner squirrel or old grub,
Time out of mind the fairies' coachmakers.
And in this state she gallops night by night
Through lovers' brains, and then they dream of love;
Over courtiers' knees, that dream on curtsies straight;
Over lawyers' fingers, who straight dream on fees;
Over ladies' lips, who straight on kisses dream,
Which often the angry Mab with blisters plagues,
Because their breaths with sweetmeats tainted are.
Sometime she gallops over a courtier's nose,
And then dreams he of smelling out a suit;
And sometime comes she with a tithe-pig's tail
Tickling a parson's nose as 'a lies asleep,
Then dreams he of another benefice.
Sometimes she drives over a soldier's neck,
And then dreams he of cutting foreign throats,
Of breaches, ambuscadoes, Spanish blades,
Of healths five fathom deep; and then anon
Drums in his ear, at which he starts and wakes,
And being thus frighted, swears a prayer or two
And sleeps again. This is that very Mab
That plaits the manes of horses in the night
And bakes the elflocks in foul sluttish hairs,
Which once untangled much misfortune bodes
This is the hag, when maids lie on their backs,
That presses them and learns them first to bear,
Making them women of good carriage.
This is she—

Romeo: Peace, peace, Mercutio, peace!
You talk of nothing.

Mercutio: True, I talk of dreams;
Which are the children of an idle brain,
Begot of nothing but vain fantasy;
Which is as thin of substance as the air,
And more inconstant than the wind, who wooes
Even now the frozen bosom of the North
And, being angered, puffs away from thence,
Turning his face to the dew-dropping South.

Benvolio: This wind you talk of blows us from ourselves.
Supper is done, and we shall come too late.

Romeo: I fear, too early; for my mind misgives
Some consequence, yet hanging in the stars,
Shall bitterly begin his fearful date
With this night's revels and expire the term
Of a despised life, closed in my breast,
By some vile forfeit of untimely death.
But he that has the steerage of my course
Direct my sail! On, lusty gentlemen!

Benvolio: Strike, drum.

[*They march about the stage. Exit*]

my mind misgives
Some consequence, yet hanging in the stars

5

[Capulet's house]

[Servants with napkins]

First Servant: Where's Potpan, that he helps not to take away? He shift a trencher! he scrape a trencher!

Second Servant: When good manners shall lie all in one or two men's hands, and they unwashed too, 'tis a foul thing.

First Servant: Away with the join-stools, remove the court-cubbert, look to the plate. Good you, save me a piece of marchpane and, as you love me, let the porter let in Susan Grindstone and Nell. Anthony, and Potpan!

Second Servant: Ay, boy, ready.

First Servant: You are looked for and called for, asked for and sought for, in the great chamber.

Third Servant: We cannot be here and there too. Cheerly, boys! Be brisk awhile, and the longer liver take all.

[Exit]

[Enter Masqueraders, Servants, Capulet, Lady Capulet, Juliet, Tybalt, and Guests]

Capulet: Welcome, gentlemen! Ladies that have their toes
Unplagued with corns will have a bout with you.
Ah ha, my mistresses! which of you all
Will now deny to dance? She that makes dainty,
She I'll swear has corns. Am I come near ye now?
Welcome, gentlemen! I have seen the day
That I have worn a visor and could tell
A whispering tale in a fair lady's ear,
Such as would please. 'Tis gone, 'tis gone, 'tis gone!
You are welcome, gentlemen! Come, musicians, play.
A hall, a hall! give room! and foot it, girls.

[Music plays, and they dance]

More light, you knaves! and turn the tables up,
And quench the fire, the room is grown too hot.
Ah, sirrah, this unlooked-for sport comes well.
Nay, sit, nay, sit, good cousin Capulet,
For you and I are past our dancing days.

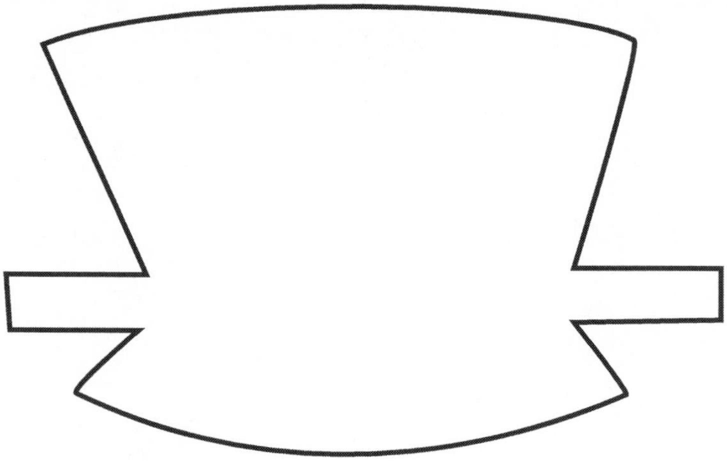

How long is it now since last yourself and I
Were in a mask?

Capulet cousin: By your Lady, thirty years.

Capulet: What, man? 'tis not so much, 'tis not so much!
'Tis since the nuptial of Lucentio,
Come Pentecost as quickly as it will,
Some five-and-twenty years, and then we masked.

Capulet cousin: 'tis more, 'tis more! His son is elder, sir;
His son is thirty.

Capulet: Will you tell me that?
His son was but a ward two years ago.

A hall, a hall! give room! and foot it, girls.

Romeo: [*to a Servant*] What lady's that, which does enrich the hand
Of yonder knight?

Servant: I know not, sir.

Romeo: O, she does teach the torches to burn bright!
It seems she hangs upon the cheek of night
Like a rich jewel in an Ethiop's ear—
Beauty too rich for use, for earth too dear!
So shows a snowy dove trooping with crows
As yonder lady over her fellows shows.
The measure done, I'll watch her place of stand
And, touching hers, make blessed my rude hand.
Did my heart love till now? Forswear it, sight!
For I never saw true beauty till this night.

Tybalt: This, by his voice, should be a Montague.
Fetch me my rapier, boy. What, dares the slave
Come here, covered with an antic face,
To fleer and scorn at our solemnity?
Now, by the stock and honor of my kin,
To strike him dead I hold it not a sin.

Capulet: Why, how now, kinsman? Wherefore storm you so?

Tybalt: Uncle, this is a Montague, our foe;
A villain, that is here come in spite
To scorn at our solemnity this night.

Capulet: Young Romeo is it?

Tybalt: 'Tis he, that villain Romeo.

Capulet: Content you, gentle cuz, let him alone.
'A bears him like a portly gentleman,
And, to say truth, Verona brags of him
To be a virtuous and well-governed youth.
I would not for the wealth of all this town
Here in my house do him disparagement.
Therefore be patient, take no note of him.
It is my will; the which if you respect,
Show a fair presence and put off these frowns,
An ill-beseeming semblance for a feast.

Tybalt: It fits when such a villain is a guest.
I'll not endure him.

Capulet: He shall be endured.
What, goodman boy? I say he shall. Go to!
Am I the master here, or you? Go to!
You'll not endure him? God shall mend my soul!
You'll make a mutiny among my guests!
You will set cock-a-hoop! you'll be the man!

Tybalt: Why, uncle, 'tis a shame.

Capulet: Go to, go to!
You are a saucy boy. Is it so, indeed?
This trick may chance to scathe you. I know what.
You must contrary me! Indeed, 'tis time.—

This, by his voice, should be a Montague.

Well said, my hearts!— You are a princox— go!
Be quiet, or— More light, more light!— For shame!
I'll make you quiet; what!— Cheerly, my hearts!

Tybalt: Patience perforce with wilful choler meeting
Makes my flesh tremble in their different greeting.
I will withdraw; but this intrusion shall,
Now seeming sweet, convert to bitterest gall.

[*Exit*]

Romeo: If I profane with my unworthiest hand
This holy shrine, the gentle fine is this:
My lips, two blushing pilgrims, ready stand
To smooth that rough touch with a tender kiss.

Juliet: Good pilgrim, you do wrong your hand too much,
Which mannerly devotion shows in this;
For saints have hands that pilgrims' hands do touch,
And palm to palm is holy palmers' kiss.

Romeo: Have not saints lips, and holy palmers too?

Juliet:Yes, pilgrim, lips that they must use in prayer.

Romeo: O, then, dear saint, let lips do what hands do!
They pray; grant you, lest faith turn to despair.

Juliet: Saints do not move, though grant for prayers' sake.

Romeo: Then move not while my prayer's effect I take.
Thus from my lips, by yours my sin is purged.

[*Kisses her*]

Juliet: Then have my lips the sin that they have took.

Romeo: Sin from my lips? O trespass sweetly urged!
Give me my sin again.

[*Kisses her*]

Juliet: You kiss by the book.

[*Nurse interrupts*]

Nurse: Madam, your mother craves a word with you.

[*Juliet hurries to her mother*]

Romeo: What is her mother?

Nurse: Indeed, bachelor,
Her mother is the lady of the house.
And a good lady, and a wise and virtuous.
I nursed her daughter that you talked withal.
I tell you, he that can lay hold of her
Shall have the chinks.

Romeo: Is she a Capulet?
O dear account! my life is my foe's debt.

Benvolio: Away, be gone; the sport is at the best.

Romeo: Yes, so I fear; the more is my unrest.

Capulet: Nay, gentlemen, prepare not to be gone;
We have a trifling foolish banquet towards.
Is it even so? Why then, I thank you all.
I thank you, honest gentlemen. Good night.
More torches here!

[*Exit Maskers*]

Come on then, let's to bed.
Ah, sirrah, by my fay, it waxes late;
I'll to my rest.

[*Exit all but Juliet and Nurse*]

You kiss by the book.

Juliet: Come here, Nurse. What is yond gentleman?

Nurse: The son and heir of old Tiberio.

Juliet: What's he that now is going out of door?

Nurse: Surely, that, I think, be young Petruchio.

Juliet: What's he that follows there, that would not dance?

Nurse: I know not.

Juliet: Go ask his name.— If he be married,
My grave is like to be my wedding bed.

[*Nurse goes and comes back*]

Nurse: His name is Romeo, and a Montague,
The only son of your great enemy.

Juliet: My only love, sprung from my only hate!
Too early seen unknown, and known too late!
Prodigious birth of love it is to me
That I must love a loathed enemy.

Nurse: What's this? what's this?

Juliet: A rhyme I learned even now
Of one I danced withal.

[*One calls within, "Juliet."*]

Nurse: Anon, anon!
Come, let's away; the strangers all are gone.

[*Exit*]

My only love, sprung from my only hate!

Prologue

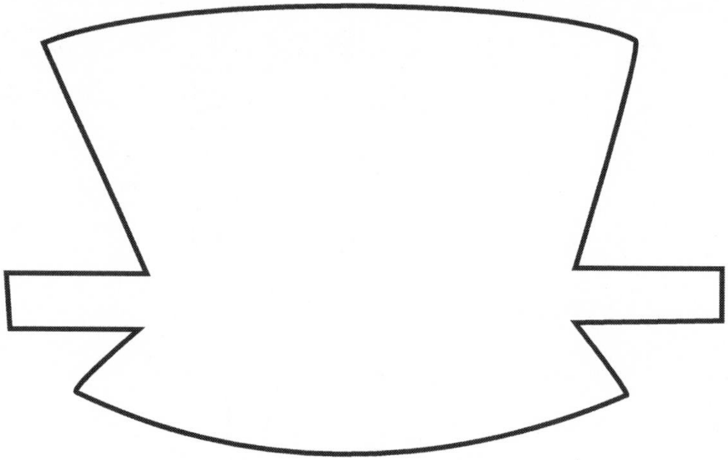

[*Enter Announcer*]

Announcer: Now old desire does in his deathbed lie,
And young affection gapes to be his heir;
That fair for which love groaned for and would die,
With tender Juliet matched, is now not fair.
Now Romeo is beloved, and loves again,
Alike bewitched by the charm of looks;
But to his foe supposed he must complain,
And she steal love's sweet bait from fearful hooks.
Being held a foe, he may not have access
To breathe such vows as lovers use to swear,
And she as much in love, her means much less
To meet her new beloved anywhere;
But passion lends them power, time, means, to meet,
Tempering extremities with extreme sweet.

[*Exit*]

Now Romeo is beloved, and loves again

Act Two

1

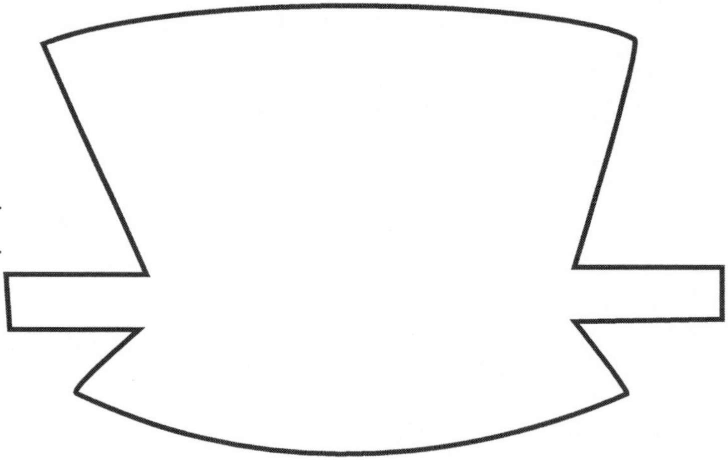

[A lane by the wall of Capulet's orchard]

[Enter Romeo alone]

Romeo: Can I go forward when my heart is here?
Turn back, dull earth, and find your center out.

[Climbs the wall and leaps over it]

[Enter Benvolio with Mercutio]

Benvolio: Romeo! my cousin Romeo! Romeo!

Mercutio: He is wise,
And, on my life, has stolen him home to bed.

Benvolio: He ran this way, and leapt this orchard wall.
Call, good Mercutio.

Mercutio: Nay, I'll conjure too.
Romeo! humors! madman! passion! lover!
Appear you in the likeness of a sigh;
Speak but one rhyme, and I am satisfied!
Cry but "Ay me!" pronounce but "love" and "dove";
Speak to my gossip Venus one fair word,
One nickname for her purblind son and heir,
Young Adam Cupid, he that shot so trim
When King Cophetua loved the beggar maid!
He hears not, he stirs not, he moves not;
The ape is dead, and I must conjure him.
I conjure you by Rosaline's bright eyes.
By her high forehead and her scarlet lip,
By her fine foot, straight leg, and quivering thigh,
And the demesnes that there adjacent lie,
That in your likeness you appear to us!

Benvolio: Though if he hear you, you will anger him.

Mercutio: This cannot anger him. 'Twould anger him
To raise a spirit in his mistress' circle
Of some strange nature, letting it there stand
Till she had laid it and conjured it down.
That were some spite; my invocation
Is fair and honest: in his mistress' name,
I conjure only but to raise up him.

Benvolio: Come, he has hid himself among these trees
To be consorted with the hormonal night.
Blind is his love and best befits the dark.

Mercutio: If love be blind, love cannot hit the mark.
Now will he sit under a medlar tree
And wish his mistress were that kind of fruit
As maids call medlars when they laugh alone.
O, Romeo, that she were, O that she were
An open et cetera, you a poperin pear!
Romeo, good night. I'll to my truckle-bed;
This field-bed is too cold for me to sleep.
Come, shall we go?

Benvolio: Go then, for 'tis in vain
To seek him here that means not to be found.

[*Exit*]

2

[Capulet's orchard]

[Enter Romeo]

Romeo: He jests at scars that never felt a wound.

[Enter Juliet above at a window]

But soft! What light through yonder window breaks?
It is the East, and Juliet is the sun!
Arise, fair sun, and kill the envious moon,
Who is already sick and pale with grief
That you, her maid, are far more fair than she.
Be not her maid, since she is envious.
Her vestal livery is but sick and green,
And none but fools do wear it. Cast it off.
It is my lady; O, it is my love!
O that she knew she were!
She speaks, yet she says nothing. What of that?
Her eye discourses; I will answer it.
I am too bold; 'tis not to me she speaks.
Two of the fairest stars in all the heaven,
Having some business, do entreat her eyes
To twinkle in their spheres till they return.
What if her eyes were there, they in her head?
The brightness of her cheek would shame those stars
As daylight does a lamp; her eyes in heaven
Would through the airy region stream so bright
That birds would sing and think it were not night.
See how she leans her cheek upon her hand!
O that I were a glove upon that hand,
That I might touch that cheek!

Juliet: Ay me!

Romeo: She speaks.
O, speak again, bright angel! for you are
As glorious to this night, being over my head,
As is a winged messenger of heaven
Unto the white-upturned wondering eyes
Of mortals that fall back to gaze on him
When he bestrides the lazy-pacing clouds
And sails upon the bosom of the air.

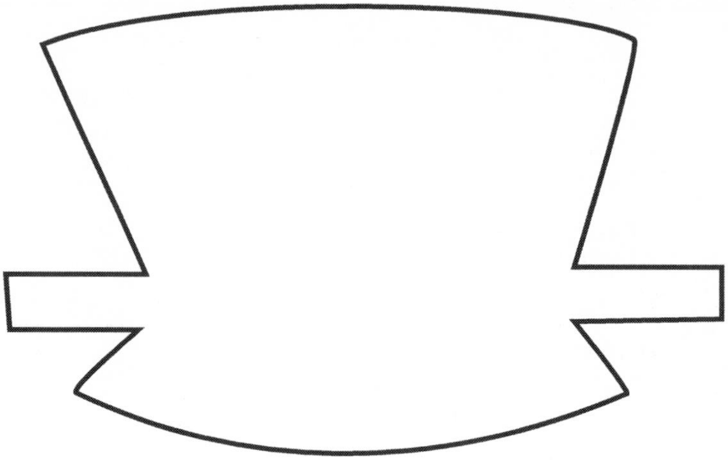

Juliet: O Romeo, Romeo! where are you Romeo?
Deny your father and refuse your name!
Or, if you will not, be but sworn my love,
And I'll no longer be a Capulet.

Romeo: [*aside*] Shall I hear more, or shall I speak at this?

Juliet: 'Tis but your name that is my enemy.
You are yourself, though not a Montague.
What's Montague? it is nor hand, nor foot,
Nor arm, nor face, nor any other part
Belonging to a man. O, be some other name!
What's in a name? That which we call a rose
By any other name would smell as sweet.
So Romeo would, were he not Romeo called,
Retain that dear perfection which he owes
Without that title. Romeo, doff your name;
And for that name, which is no part of you,
Take all myself.

Romeo: I take you at your word.
Call me but love, and I'll be new baptized;
Henceforth I never will be Romeo.

Juliet: What man are you that, thus bescreened in night,
So stumbles on my counsel?

Romeo: By a name
I know not how to tell you who I am.
My name, dear saint, is hateful to myself,
Because it is an enemy to you.
Had I it written, I would tear the word.

Juliet: My ears have yet not drunk a hundred words
Of that tongue's utterance, yet I know the sound.
Are you not Romeo, and a Montague?

Romeo: Neither, fair saint, if either you dislike.

Juliet: How came you here, tell me, and what for?
The orchard walls are high and hard to climb,
And the place—death, considering who you are,
If any of my kinsmen find you here.

Romeo: With love's light wings did I overperch these walls;
For stony limits cannot hold love out,
And what love can do, that dares love attempt.
Therefore your kinsmen are no block to me.

Juliet: If they do see you, they will murder you.

Romeo: Alack, there lies more peril in your eye
Than twenty of their swords! Look you but sweet,
And I am proof against their enmity.

Juliet: I would not for the world they saw you here.

Romeo: I have night's cloak to hide me from their sight;
And but you love me, let them find me here.
My life were better ended by their hate
Than death postponed, wanting of your love.

Are you not Romeo, and a Montague?

Juliet: By whose direction found you out this place?

Romeo: By love, that first did prompt me to enquire.
He lent me counsel, and I lent him eyes.
I am no pilot; yet, were you as far
As that vast shore washed with the farthest sea,
I would adventure for such merchandise.

Juliet: You know the mask of night is on my face;
Else would a maiden blush bepaint my cheek
For that which you have heard me speak tonight.
Fain would I dwell on form— fain, fain deny
What I have spoke; but farewell compliment!
Do you love me, I know you will say "Ay";
And I will take your word. Yet, if you swear,
You may prove false. At lovers' perjuries,
They say Jove laughs. O gentle Romeo,
If you do love, pronounce it faithfully.
Or if you think I am too quickly won,
I'll frown, and be perverse, and say you nay,
So you will woo; but else, not for the world.
In truth, fair Montague, I am too fond,
And therefore you may think my behavior light;
But trust me, gentleman, I'll prove more true
Than those that have more cunning to be strange.
I should have been more strange, I must confess,
But that you overheard, before I was aware,
My true-love passion. Therefore pardon me,
And not impute this yielding to light love,
Which the dark night has so discovered.

Romeo: Lady, by yonder blessed moon I swear,
That tips with silver all these fruit-tree tops—

Juliet: O, swear not by the moon, the inconstant moon,
That monthly changes in her circled orb,
Lest that your love prove likewise variable.

Romeo: What shall I swear by?

Juliet: Do not swear at all;
Or if you will, swear by your gracious self,
Which is the god of my idolatry,
And I'll believe you.

Romeo: If my heart's dear love—

Juliet: Well, do not swear. Although I joy in you,
I have no joy of this contract tonight.
It is too rash, too unadvised, too sudden;
Too like the lightning, which does cease to be
Before one can say "It lightens." Sweet, good night!
This bud of love, by summer's ripening breath,
May prove a beauteous flower when next we meet.
Good night, good night! As sweet repose and rest
Come to your heart as that within my breast!

Romeo: O, will you leave me so unsatisfied?

O, swear not by the moon, the inconstant moon

Juliet: What satisfaction can you have tonight?

Romeo: The exchange of your love's faithful vow for mine.

Juliet: I gave you mine before you did request it;
And yet I would it were to give again.

Romeo: Would you withdraw it? For what purpose, love?

Juliet: But to be frank and give it you again.
And yet I wish but for the thing I have.
My bounty is as boundless as the sea,
My love as deep; the more I give to you,
The more I have, for both are infinite.
I hear some noise within. Dear love, adieu!

[*Nurse calls within*]

Anon, good nurse! Sweet Montague, be true.
Stay but a little, I will come again.

[*Exit*]

Romeo: O blessed, blessed night! I am afraid,
Being in night, all this is but a dream,
Too flattering-sweet to be substantial.

[*Enter Juliet above*]

Juliet: Three words, dear Romeo, and good night indeed.
If that your bent of love be honorable,
Your purpose marriage, send me word tomorrow,
By one that I'll procure to come to you,
Where and what time you will perform the rite;
And all my fortunes at your foot I'll lay
And follow you my lord throughout the world.

Nurse: [*within*] Madam!

Juliet: I come, anon.— But if you mean not well,
I do beseech you—

Nurse: [*within*] Madam!

Juliet: By-and-by I come.—
To cease your suit and leave me to my grief.
Tomorrow will I send.

Romeo: So thrive my soul—

Juliet: A thousand times good night!

[*Exit Juliet*]

My bounty is as boundless as the sea,
My love as deep

Romeo: A thousand times the worse, to want your light!
Love goes toward love as schoolboys from their books;
But love from love, towards school with heavy looks.

[*Enter Juliet again*]

Juliet: Hist! Romeo, hist! O for a falconer's voice
To lure this tassel-gentle back again!
Bondage is hoarse and may not speak aloud;
Else would I tear the cave where Echo lies,
And make her airy tongue more hoarse than mine
With repetition of my Romeo's name.
Romeo!

Romeo: It is my soul that calls upon my name.
How silver-sweet sound lovers' tongues by night,
Like softest music to attending ears!

Juliet: Romeo!

Romeo: My dear?

Juliet: At what o'clock tomorrow
Shall I send to you?

Romeo: By the hour of nine.

Juliet: I will not fail. 'Tis twenty years till then.
I have forgot why I did call you back.

Romeo: Let me stand here till you remember it.

Juliet: I shall forget, to have you still stand there,
Remembering how I love your company.

Romeo: And I'll still stay, to have you still forget,
Forgetting any other home but this.

Juliet: 'Tis almost morning. I would have you gone—
And yet no farther than a wanton's bird,
That lets it hop a little from her hand,
Like a poor prisoner in his twisted gyves,
And with a silk thread plucks it back again,
So loving-jealous of his liberty.

Romeo: I would I were your bird.

Juliet: Sweet, so would I.
Yet I should kill you with much cherishing.
Good night, good night! Parting is such sweet sorrow,
That I shall say good night till it be morrow.

[*Exit*]

Romeo: Sleep dwell upon your eyes, peace in your breast!
Would I were sleep and peace, so sweet to rest!
Hence will I to my ghostly father's cell,
His help to crave and my dear hap to tell.

[*Exit*]

3

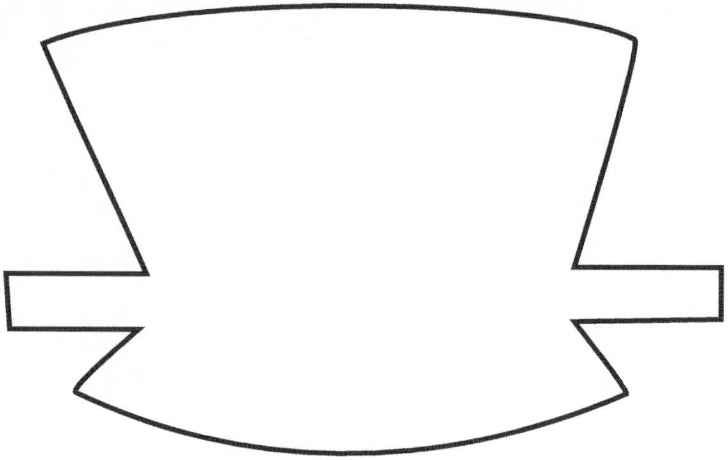

[Friar Laurence's cell]

[Enter Friar Laurence alone, with a basket]

Friar Laurence: The gray-eyed morn smiles on the frowning night,
Checkering the Eastern clouds with streaks of light;
And flecked darkness like a drunkard reels
From forth day's path and Titan's fiery wheels.
Now, before the sun advance his burning eye
The day to cheer and night's dank dew to dry,
I must up-fill this osier cage of ours
With baleful weeds and precious-juiced flowers.
The earth that's nature's mother is her tomb.
What is her burying grave, that is her womb;
And from her womb children of diverse kind
We sucking on her natural bosom find;
Many for many virtues excellent,
None but for some, and yet all different.
O, great is the powerful grace that lies
In plants, herbs, stones, and their true qualities;
For nothing so vile that on the earth does live
But to the earth some special good does give;
Nor any so good but, strained from that fair use,
Revolts from true birth, stumbling on abuse.
Virtue itself turns vice, being misapplied,
And vice sometimes by action dignified.
Within the infant rind of this small flower
Poison has residence, and medicine power;
For this, being smelled, with that part cheers each part;
Being tasted, slays all senses with the heart.
Two such opposed kings encamp them still
In man as well as herbs— grace and rude will;
And where the worser is predominant,
Full soon the canker death eats up that plant.

[Enter Romeo]

Romeo: Good morrow, father.

Friar Laurence: Benedicite!
What early tongue so sweet salutes me?
Young son, it argues a distempered head
So soon to bid good morrow to your bed.
Care keeps his watch in every old man's eye,
And where care lodges sleep will never lie;
But where unbruised youth with unstuffed brain
Does couch his limbs, there golden sleep does reign.
Therefore your earliness does me assure
You are uproused with some intemperateness;
Or if not so, then here I hit it right—
Our Romeo has not been in bed tonight.

Romeo: That last is true—the sweeter rest was mine.

Our Romeo has not been in bed tonight

Friar Laurence: God pardon sin! Were you with Rosaline?

Romeo: With Rosaline, my ghostly father? No.
I have forgot that name, and that name's woe.

Friar Laurence: That's my good son! But where have you been then?

Romeo: I'll tell you before you ask it me again.
I have been feasting with my enemy,
Where on a sudden one has wounded me
That's by me wounded. Both our remedies
Within your help and holy physic lies.
I bear no hatred, blessed man, for, lo,
My intercession likewise steads my foe.

Friar Laurence: Be plain, good son, and homely in your drift
Riddling confession finds but riddling shrift.

Romeo: Then plainly know my heart's dear love is set
On the fair daughter of rich Capulet;
As mine on hers, so hers is set on mine,
And all combined, save what you must combine
By holy marriage. When, and where, and how
We met, we wooed, and made exchange of vow,
I'll tell you as we pass; but this I pray,
That you consent to marry us today.

Friar Laurence: Holy Saint Francis! What a change is here!
Is Rosaline, that you did love so dear,
So soon forsaken? Young men's love then lies
Not truly in their hearts, but in their eyes.
Jesu Maria! What a deal of brine
Has washed your sallow cheeks for Rosaline!
How much salt water thrown away in waste,
To season love, that of it does not taste!
The sun not yet your sighs from heaven clears,
Your old groans ring yet in my ancient ears.
Lo, here upon your cheek the stain does sit
Of an old tear that is not washed off yet.
If ever you were yourself, and these woes yours,
You and these woes were all for Rosaline.
And are you changed? Pronounce this sentence then:
Women may fall when there's no strength in men.

Romeo: You chided me often for loving Rosaline.

Friar Laurence: For doting, not for loving, pupil mine.

Romeo: And bade me bury love.

Friar Laurence: Not in a grave
To lay one in, another out, to have.

Romeo: I pray you chide not. She whom I love now
Does grace for grace and love for love allow.
The other did not so.

Friar Laurence: O, she knew well
Your love did read by rote, that could not spell.
But come, young waverer, come go with me.

With Rosaline...? No.
I have forgot that name, and that name's woe.

In one respect I'll your assistant be;
For this alliance may so happy prove
To turn your households' rancor to pure love.

Romeo: O, let us hence! I stand on sudden haste.

Friar Laurence: Wisely, and slow. They stumble that run fast.

[*Exit*]

4

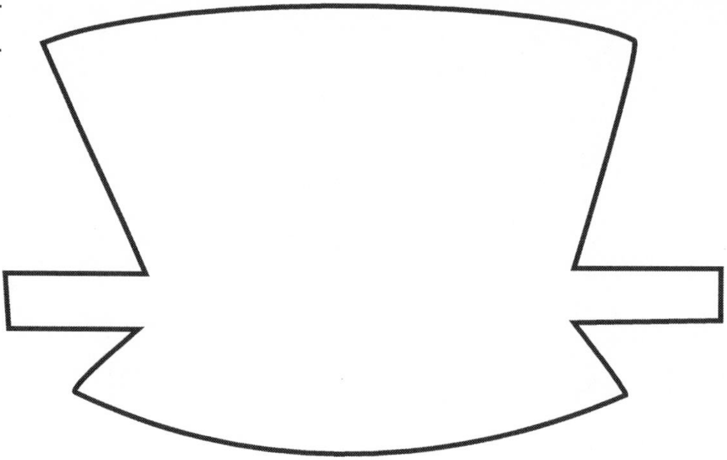

[*A street*]

[*Enter Benvolio and Mercutio*]

Mercutio: Where the devil should this Romeo be?
Came he not home tonight?

Benvolio: Not to his father's. I spoke with his man.

Mercutio: Why, that same pale hard-hearted wench, that Rosaline,
Torments him so that he will sure run mad.

Benvolio: Tybalt, the kinsman to old Capulet,
Has sent a letter to his father's house.

Mercutio: A challenge, on my life.

Benvolio: Romeo will answer it.

Mercutio: Any man that can write may answer a letter.

Benvolio: Nay, he will answer the letter's master, how he dares, being dared.

Mercutio: Alas, poor Romeo, he is already dead! Stabbed with a white wench's black eye; shot through the ear with a love song; the very pin of his heart cleft with the blind bow-boy's butt-shaft; and is he a man to encounter Tybalt?

Benvolio: Why, what is Tybalt?

Mercutio: More than Prince of Cats, I can tell you. O, he's the courageous captain of compliments. He fights as you sing pricksong—keeps time, distance, and proportion; rests me his minim rest, one, two, and the third in your bosom! the very butcher of a silk button, a duellist, a duellist! a gentleman of the very first house, of the first and second cause. Ah, the immortal passado! the punto reverse! the hay.

Benvolio: The what?

Mercutio: The pox of such antic, lisping, affecting fantasticoes— these new tuners of accent! "By Jesu, a very good blade! a very tall man! a very good whore!" Why, is not this a lamentable thing, grandsir, that we should be thus afflicted with these strange flies, these fashion-mongers, these pardona-mi's, who stand so much on the new form that they cannot sit at ease on the old bench? O, their bones, their bones!

[*Enter Romeo*]

Why, what is Tybalt?

Benvolio: Here comes Romeo! here comes Romeo!

Mercutio: Without his roe, like a dried herring. O flesh, flesh, how are you fishified! Now is he for the numbers that Petrarch flowed in. Laura, to his lady, was but a kitchen wench (indeed, she had a better love to berhyme her), Dido a dowdy, Cleopatra a gypsy, Helen and Hero hildings and harlots, This be a gray eye or so, but not to the purpose. Signior Romeo, bon jour! There's a French salutation to your French slop. You gave us the counterfeit fairly last night.

Romeo: Good morrow to you both. What counterfeit did I give you?

Mercutio: The slip, sir, the slip. Can you not conceive?

Romeo: Pardon, good Mercutio. My business was great, and in such a case as mine a man may strain courtesy.

Mercutio: That's as much as to say, such a case as yours constrains a man to bow in the hams.

Romeo: Meaning, to curtsy.

Mercutio: You have most kindly hit it.

Romeo: A most courteous exposition.

Mercutio: Nay, I am the very pink of courtesy.

Romeo: Pink for flower.

Mercutio: Right.

Romeo: Why, then is my pump well-flowered.

Mercutio: Well said! Follow me this jest now till you have worn out your pump, that, when the single sole of it is worn, the jest may remain, after the wearing, solely singular.

Romeo: O single-sold jest, solely singular for the singleness!

Mercutio: Come between us, good Benvolio! My wits faint.

Romeo: Switches and spurs, switches and spurs! or I'll cry a match.

Mercutio: Nay, if our wits run the wild-goose chase, I am done; for you have more of the wild goose in one of your wits than, I am sure, I have in my whole five. Was I with you there for the goose?

Romeo: You were never with me for anything when you were not there for the goose.

Come between us, good Benvolio! My wits faint.

Mercutio: I will bite you by the ear for that jest.

Romeo: Nay, good goose, bite not!

Mercutio: Your wit is a very bitter sweeting; it is a most sharp sauce.

Romeo: And is it not, then, well served in to a sweet goose?

Mercutio: O, here's a wit of cheveril, that stretches from an inch narrow to an ell broad!

Romeo: I stretch it out for that word "broad," which, added to the goose, proves you far and wide a broad goose.

Mercutio: Why, is not this better now than groaning for love? Now are you sociable, now are you Romeo; now are you what you are, by art as well as by nature. For this drivelling love is like a great natural that runs lolling up and down to hide his bauble in a hole.

Benvolio: Stop there, stop there!

Mercutio: You desire me to stop in my tale against the hair.

Benvolio: You would else have made your tale large.

Mercutio: O, you are deceived! I would have made it short; for I was come to the whole depth of my tale, and meant indeed to occupy the argument no longer.

Romeo: Here's goodly gear!

Why, is not this better now than groaning for love?

[*Enter Nurse and Peter*]

Mercutio: A sail, a sail!

Benvolio: Two, two! a shirt and a smock.

Nurse: Peter!

Peter: Anon.

Nurse: My fan, Peter.

Mercutio: Good Peter, to hide her face; for her fan's the fairer face of the two.

Nurse: God ye good morrow, gentlemen.

Mercutio: God ye good day, fair gentlewoman.

Nurse: Is it good day?

Mercutio: 'Tis no less, I tell you; for the bawdy hand of the dial is now upon the prick of noon.

Nurse: Out upon you! What a man are you!

Romeo: One, gentlewoman, that God has made for himself to mar.

Nurse: By my troth, it is well said. "For himself to mar," quoth 'a? Gentlemen, can any of you tell me where I may find the young Romeo?

Romeo: I can tell you; but young Romeo will be older when you have found him than he was when you sought him. I am the youngest of that name, for fault of a worse.

Nurse: You say well.

Mercutio: Yea, is the worst well? Very well took, in faith! wisely, wisely.

Nurse: If you be he, sir, I desire some confidence with you.

Benvolio: She will endite him to some supper.

Mercutio: A bawd, a bawd, a bawd! So ho!

Romeo: What have you found?

Mercutio: No hare, sir; unless a hare, sir, in a lenten pie, that is something stale and hoar before it be spent

[*He walks by them and sings*]

An old hare hoar,
And an old hare hoar,
Is very good meat in Lent;
But a hare that is hoar
Is too much for a score
When it hoars before it be spent.

Romeo, will you come to your father's? We'll to dinner there.

Romeo: I will follow you.

Mercutio: Farewell, ancient lady. Farewell, [sings] lady, lady, lady.

[*Exit Mercutio, Benvolio*]

the bawdy hand of the dial is now upon the prick of noon

Nurse: Well then, farewell! I Pray you, Sir, what saucy merchant was this that was so full of his ropery?

Romeo: A gentleman, nurse, that loves to hear himself talk and will speak more in a minute than he will stand to in a month.

Nurse: If 'a speak anything against me, I'll take him down, if 'a were lustier than he is, and twenty such jacks; and if I cannot, I'll find those that shall. Scurvy knave! I am none of his flirt-gills; I am none of his skains-mates. And you must stand by too, and suffer every knave to use me at his pleasure!

Peter: I saw no man use you at his pleasure. If I had, my weapon should quickly have been out, I warrant you. I dare draw as soon as another man, if I see occasion in a good quarrel, and the law on my side.

Nurse: Now, afore God, I am so vexed that every part about me quivers. Scurvy knave! Pray you, sir, a word; and, as I told you, my young lady bid me enquire you out. What she bid me say, I will keep to myself; but first let me tell ye, if ye should lead her into a fool's paradise, as they say, it were a very gross kind of behavior, as they say; for the gentlewoman is young; and therefore, if you should deal double with her, truly it were an ill thing to be offered to any gentlewoman, and very weak dealing.

Romeo: Nurse, commend me to your lady and mistress. I protest unto you—

Nurse: Good heart, and in faith I will tell her as much. Lord, Lord! she will be a joyful woman.

Romeo: What will you tell her, nurse? you do not mark me.

Nurse: I will tell her, sir, that you do protest, which, as I take it, is a gentlemanlike offer.

Romeo: Bid her devise
Some means to come to shrift this afternoon;
And there she shall at Friar Laurence's cell
Be shrived and married. Here is for your pains.

Nurse: No, truly, sir; not a penny.

Romeo: Go to! I say you shall.

Nurse: This afternoon, sir? Well, she shall be there.

Romeo: And stay, good nurse, behind the abbey wall.
Within this hour my man shall be with you
And bring you cords made like a tackled stair,
Which to the high topgallant of my joy
Must be my convoy in the secret night.
Farewell. Be trusty, and I'll quit your pains.
Farewell. Commend me to your mistress.

my young lady bid me enquire you out

Nurse: Now God in heaven bless you! Hark you, sir.

Romeo: What say you, my dear nurse?

Nurse: Is your man secret? Did you never hear say,
Two may keep counsel, putting one away?

Romeo: I warrant you my man's as true as steel.

Nurse: Well, sir, my mistress is the sweetest lady. Lord, Lord! when 'twas a little prating thing— O, there is a nobleman in town, one Paris, that would fain lay knife aboard; but she, good soul, had as lief see a toad, a very toad, as see him. I anger her sometimes, and tell her that Paris is the properer man; but I'll warrant you, when I say so, she looks as pale as any clout in the versal world. Does not rosemary and Romeo begin both with a letter?

Romeo: Yes, nurse; what of that? Both with an R.

Nurse: Ah, mocker! that's the dog's name. R is for the— No; I know it begins with some other letter; and she has the prettiest sententious of it, of you and rosemary, that it would do you good to hear it.

Romeo: Commend me to your lady.

Nurse: Ay, a thousand times.

[*Exit Romeo*]

Peter!

Peter: Anon.

Nurse: Peter, take my fan, and go before, and apace.

[*Exit*]

Well, sir, my mistress is the sweetest lady

5

[*Capulet's orchard*]

[*Enter Juliet*]

Juliet: The clock struck nine when I did send the nurse;
In half an hour she promised to return.
Perchance she cannot meet him. That's not so.
O, she is lame! Love's heralds should be thoughts,
Which ten times faster glide than the sun's beams
Driving back shadows over lowering hills.
Therefore do nimble-pinioned doves draw Love,
And therefore has the wind-swift Cupid wings.
Now is the sun upon the highmost hill
Of this day's journey, and from nine till twelve
Is three long hours; yet she is not come.
Had she affections and warm youthful blood,
She would be as swift in motion as a ball;
My words would bandy her to my sweet love,
And his to me,
But old folks, many feign as they were dead—
Unwieldy, slow, heavy and pale as lead.

[*Enter Nurse and Peter*]

O God, she comes! O honey nurse, what news?
Have you met with him? Send your man away.

Nurse: Peter, stay at the gate.

[*Exit Peter*]

Juliet: Now, good sweet nurse— O Lord, why look you sad?
Though news be sad, yet tell them merrily;
If good, you shame the music of sweet news
By playing it to me with so sour a face.

Nurse: I am aweary, give me leave awhile.
Fie, how my bones ache! What a jounce have I had!

Juliet: I would you had my bones, and I your news.
Nay, come, I pray you speak. Good, good nurse, speak.

Nurse: Jesu, what haste! Can you not stay awhile?
Do you not see that I am out of breath?

Juliet: How are you out of breath when you have breath
To say to me that you are out of breath?
The excuse that you do make in this delay

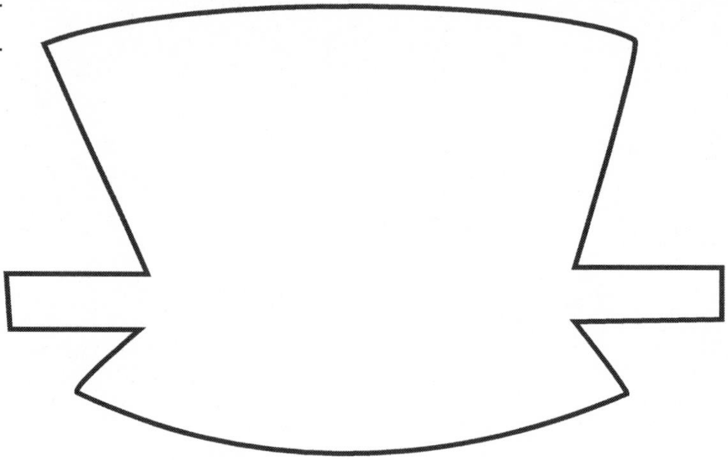

Is longer than the tale you do excuse.
Is your news good or bad? Answer to that.
Say either, and I'll stay the circumstance.
Let me be satisfied, is it good or bad?

three long hours; yet she is not come

Nurse: Well, you have made a simple choice; you know not how to choose a man. Romeo? No, not he. Though his face be better than any man's, yet his leg excels all men's; and for a hand and a foot, and a body, though they be not to be talked on, yet they are past compare. He is not the flower of courtesy, but, I'll warrant him, as gentle as a lamb. Go your ways, wench; serve God. What, have you dined at home?

Juliet: No, no. But all this did I know before.
What says he of our marriage? What of that?

Nurse: Lord, how my head aches! What a head have I!
It beats as it would fall in twenty pieces.
My back on the other side,— ah, my back, my back!
Beshrew your heart for sending me about
To catch my death with jouncing up and down!

Juliet: In faith, I am sorry that you are not well.
Sweet, sweet, sweet nurse, tell me, what says my love?

Nurse: Your love says, like an honest gentleman, and a courteous, and a kind, and a handsome; and, I warrant, a virtuous— Where is your mother?

Juliet: Where is my mother? Why, she is within.
Where should she be? How oddly you reply!
Your love says, like an honest gentleman,
"Where is your mother?"

Nurse: O God's Lady dear!
Are you so hot? Indeed come up, I think.
Is this the poultice for my aching bones?
Henceforward do your messages yourself.

Juliet: Here's such a coil! Come, what says Romeo?

Nurse: Have you got leave to go to shrift today?

Juliet: I have.

Nurse: Then get you hence to Friar Laurence's cell;
There stays a husband to make you a wife.
Now comes the wanton blood up in your cheeks:
They'll be in scarlet straight at any news.
Hurry you to church; I must another way,
To fetch a ladder, by which your love
Must climb a bird's nest soon when it is dark.
I am the drudge, and toil in your delight;
But you shall bear the burden soon at night.
Go; I'll to dinner; hie you to the cell.

Juliet: Hie to high fortune! Honest nurse, farewell.

[*Exit*]

ah, my back, my back!
Beshrew your heart for sending me about

6

[*Friar Laurence's cell*]

[*Enter Friar Laurence and Romeo*]

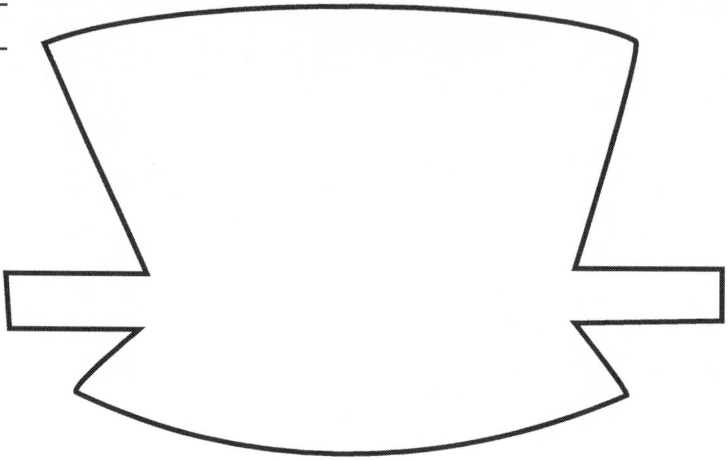

Friar Laurence: So smile the heavens upon this holy act
That after-hours with sorrow chide us not!

Romeo: Amen, amen! But come what sorrow can,
It cannot countervail the exchange of joy
That one short minute gives me in her sight.
Do you but close our hands with holy words,
Then love-devouring death do what he dare—
It is enough I may but call her mine.

Friar Laurence: These violent delights have violent ends
And in their triumph die, like fire and powder,
Which, as they kiss, consume. The sweetest honey
Is loathsome in his own deliciousness
And in the taste confounds the appetite.
Therefore love moderately: long love does so;
Too swift arrives as tardy as too slow.

[*Enter Juliet*]

Here comes the lady. O, so light a foot
Will never wear out the everlasting flint.
A lover may bestride the gossamer
That idles in the wanton summer air,
And yet not fall; so light is vanity.

Juliet: Good evening to my ghostly confessor.

Friar Laurence: Romeo shall thank you, daughter, for us both.

Juliet: As much to him, else is his thanks too much.

Romeo: Ah, Juliet, if the measure of your joy
Be heaped like mine, and that your skill be more
To blazon it, then sweeten with your breath
This neighbor air, and let rich music's tongue
Unfold the imagined happiness that both
Receive in either by this dear encounter.

Juliet: Conceit, more rich in matter than in words,
Brags of his substance, not of ornament.
They are but beggars that can count their worth;
But my true love is grown to such excess
I cannot sum up sum of half my wealth.

Friar Laurence: Come, come with me, and we will make short work;
For, by your leaves, you shall not stay alone
Till Holy Church incorporate two in one.

[*Exit*]

you shall not stay alone
Till Holy Church incorporate two in one.

Act Three

1

[*A public place*]

[*Enter Mercutio, Benvolio, and ovthers*]

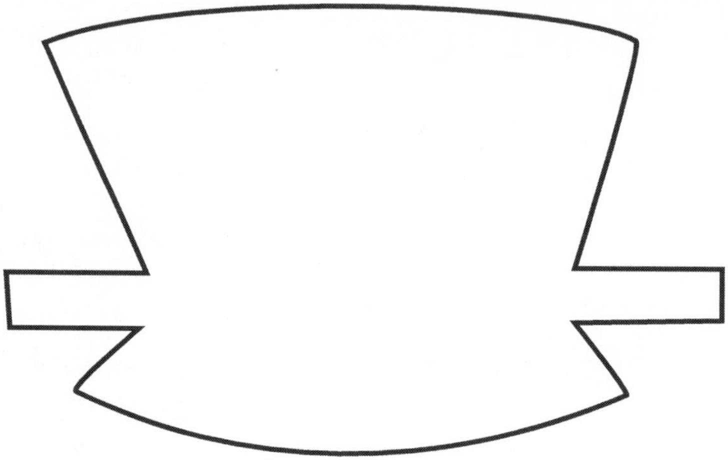

Benvolio: I pray you, good Mercutio, let's retire.
The day is hot, the Capulets abroad.
And if we meet, we shall not escape a brawl,
For now, these hot days, is the mad blood stirring.

Mercutio: You are like one of these fellows that, when he enters the confines of a tavern, claps me his sword upon the table and says "God send me no need of you!" and by the operation of the second cup draws him on the drawer, when indeed there is no need.

Benvolio: Am I like such a fellow?

Mercutio: Come, come, you are as hot a jack in your mood as any in Italy; and as soon moved to be moody, and as soon moody to be moved.

Benvolio: And what to?

Mercutio: Nay, if there were two such, we should have none shortly, for one would kill the other. You! why, you will quarrel with a man that has a hair more or a hair less in his beard than you have. You will quarrel with a man for cracking nuts, having no other reason but because you have hazel eyes. What eye but such an eye would spy out such a quarrel? your head is as full of quarrels as an egg is full of meat; and yet your head has been beaten as addle as an egg for quarrelling. you have quarrelled with a man for coughing in the street, because he has wakened your dog that has lain asleep in the sun. Did you not fall out with a tailor for wearing his new doublet before Easter, with another for tying his new shoes with an old ribbon? And yet you will tutor me from quarrelling!

Benvolio: If I were so apt to quarrel as you are, any man should buy the fee simple of my life for an hour and a quarter.

Mercutio: The fee simple? O simple!

[*Enter Tybalt and others*]

Benvolio: By my head, here come the Capulets.

Mercutio: By my heel, I care not.

Tybalt: Follow me close, for I will speak to them.
Gentlemen, good day. A word with one of you.

Mercutio: And but one word with one of us?
Couple it with something; make it a word and a blow.

Tybalt: You shall find me apt enough to that, sir, if you will give me occasion.

Mercutio: Could you not take some occasion without giving?

Tybalt: Mercutio, you consort with Romeo.

Mercutio: Consort? What, do you make us minstrels? If you make minstrels of us, look to hear nothing but discords. Here's my fiddlestick; here's that shall make you dance. Zounds, consort!

Benvolio: We talk here in the public haunt of men.
Either withdraw unto some private place
And reason coldly of your grievances,
Or else depart. Here all eyes gaze on us.

Mercutio: Men's eyes were made to look, and let them gaze.
I will not budge for no man's pleasure,

[*Enter Romeo*]

Tybalt: Well, peace be with you, sir. Here comes my man.

Mercutio: But I'll be hanged, sir, if he wear your livery.
Mark, go before to field, he'll be your follower!
Your worship in that sense may call him man.

Tybalt: Romeo, the love I bear you can afford
No better term than this: You are a villain.

Romeo: Tybalt, the reason that I have to love you
Does much excuse the appertaining rage
To such a greeting. Villain am I none.
Therefore farewell. I see you know me not.

Tybalt: Boy, this shall not excuse the injuries
That you have done me; therefore turn and draw.

Romeo: I do protest I never injured you,
But love you better than you can devise
Till you shall know the reason of my love;
And so good Capulet, which name I tender
As dearly as my own, be satisfied.

I do protest I never injured you,
But love you better than you can devise

Mercutio: O calm, dishonorable, vile submission!
Alla stoccata carries it away.

[*Draws*]

Tybalt, you ratcatcher, will you walk?

Tybalt: What would you have with me?

Mercutio: Good King of Cats, nothing but one of your nine lives. That I mean to make bold withal, and, as you shall use me hereafter, dry-beat the rest of the eight. Will you pluck your sword out of his pitcher by the ears? Make haste, lest mine be about your ears before it be out.

Tybalt: I am for you.

[*Draws*]

Romeo: Gentle Mercutio, put your rapier up.

Mercutio: Come, sir, your passado!

[*They fight*]

Romeo: Draw, Benvolio; beat down their weapons.
Gentlemen, for shame! forbear this outrage!
Tybalt, Mercutio, the Prince expressly has
Forbid this bandying in Verona streets.
Hold, Tybalt! Good Mercutio!

[*Tybalt thrusts into Mercutio, flees with his party*]

Mercutio: I am hurt.
A plague on both your houses! I am sped.
Is he gone and has nothing?

Benvolio: What, are you hurt?

Mercutio: Ay, ay, a scratch, a scratch. Ah well, 'tis enough.
Where is my page? Go, villain, fetch a surgeon.

[*Exit Page*]

Romeo: Courage, man. The hurt cannot be much.

Mercutio: No, 'tis not so deep as a well, nor so wide as a church door; but 'tis enough, 'twill serve. Ask for me tomorrow, and you shall find me a grave man. I am peppered, I warrant, for this world. A plague on both your houses! Zounds, a dog, a rat, a mouse, a cat, to scratch a man to death! a braggart, a rogue, a villain, that fights by the book of arithmetic! Why the devil came you between us? I was hurt under your arm.

Romeo: I thought all for the best.

Mercutio: Help me into some house, Benvolio,
Or I shall faint. A plague on both your houses!
They have made worms' meat of me. I have it,
And soundly too. Your houses!

[*Exit Mercutio supported by Benvolio*]

Draw, Benvolio; beat down their weapons.
Gentlemen, for shame!

Romeo: This gentleman, the Prince's near ally,
My very friend, has got this mortal hurt
In my behalf— my reputation stained
With Tybalt's slander— Tybalt, that an hour
Has been my kinsman. O sweet Juliet,
Your beauty has made me effeminate
And in my temper softened valor's steel

[*Enter Benvolio*]

Benvolio: O Romeo, Romeo, brave Mercutio's dead!
That gallant spirit has aspired the clouds,
Which too untimely here did scorn the earth.

Romeo: This day's black fate on more days does depend;
This but begins the woe others must end.

[*Enter Tybalt*]

Benvolio: Here comes the furious Tybalt back again.

Romeo: Alive in triumph, and Mercutio slain?
Away to heaven respective lenity,
And fire-eyed fury be my conduct now!
Now, Tybalt, take the "villain" back again
That late you gave me; for Mercutio's soul
Is but a little way above our heads,
Staying for yours to keep him company.
Either you or I, or both, must go with him.

Tybalt: You wretched boy, that did consort him here,
Shall with him hence.

Romeo: This shall determine that.

[*They fight. Tybalt falls*]

Benvolio: Romeo, away, be gone!
The citizens are up, and Tybalt slain.
Stand not amazed. The Prince will doom you death
If you are taken. Hence, be gone, away!

Romeo: O, I am fortune's fool!

Benvolio: Why do you stay?

[*Exit Romeo*]

O Romeo, Romeo, brave Mercutio's dead!

[Enter Citizens]

Citizen: Which way ran he that killed Mercutio?
Tybalt, that murderer, which way ran he?

Benvolio: There lies that Tybalt.

Citizen: Up, sir, go with me.
I charge you in the Prince's name obey.

[Enter Prince, Old Montague, Capulet, their Wives, and others]

Prince: Where are the vile beginners of this fray?

Benvolio: O noble Prince, I can discover all
The unlucky manage of this fatal brawl.
There lies the man, slain by young Romeo,
That slew your kinsman, brave Mercutio.

Lady Capulet: Tybalt, my cousin! O my brother's child!
O Prince! O husband! O, the blood is spilled
Of my dear kinsman! Prince, as you are true,
For blood of ours shed blood of Montague.
O cousin, cousin!

Prince: Benvolio, who began this bloody fray?

Benvolio: Tybalt, here slain, whom Romeo's hand did stay.
Romeo, that spoke him fair, bid him bethink
How nice the quarrel was, and urged withal
Your high displeasure. All this— uttered
With gentle breath, calm look, knees humbly bowed—
Could not take truce with the unruly spleen
Of Tybalt deaf to peace, but that he tilts
With piercing steel at bold Mercutio's breast;
Who, all as hot, turns deadly point to point,
And, with a martial scorn, with one hand beats
Cold death aside and with the other sends
It back to Tybalt, whose dexterity
Retorts it. Romeo he cries aloud,
"Hold, friends! friends, part!" and swifter than his
tongue,
His agile arm beats down their fatal points,
And between them rushes; underneath whose arm
An envious thrust from Tybalt hit the life
Of stout Mercutio, and then Tybalt fled;
But by-and-by comes back to Romeo,
Who had but newly entertained revenge,
And to it they go like lightning; for, before I
Could draw to part them, was stout Tybalt slain;
And, as he fell, did Romeo turn and fly.
This is the truth, or let Benvolio die.

Benvolio, who began this bloody fray?

Lady Capulet: He is a kinsman to the Montagues;
Affection makes him false, he speaks not true.
Some twenty of them fought in this black strife,
And all those twenty could but kill one life.
I beg for justice, which you, Prince, must give.
Romeo slew Tybalt; Romeo must not live.

Prince: Romeo slew him; he slew Mercutio.
Who now the price of his dear blood does owe?

Montague: Not Romeo, Prince; he was Mercutio's friend;
His fault concludes but what the law should end,
The life of Tybalt.

Prince: And for that offense
Immediately we do exile him hence.
I have an interest in your hate's proceeding,
My blood for your rude brawls does lie a-bleeding;
But I'll amerce you with so strong a fine
That you shall all repent the loss of mine.
I will be deaf to pleading and excuses;
Nor tears nor prayers shall purchase out abuses.
Therefore use none. Let Romeo flee in haste,
Else, when he is found, that hour is his last.
Bear away this body, and attend our will.
Mercy but murders, pardoning those that kill.

[*Exit*]

Romeo slew him; he slew Mercutio.
Who now the price of his dear blood does owe?

2

[*Capulet's orchard*]

[*Enter Juliet alone*]

Juliet: Gallop apace, you fiery-footed steeds,
Towards Phoebus' lodging! Such a wagoner
As Phaeton would whip you to the West
And bring in cloudy night immediately.
Spread your close curtain, love-performing night,
That runaway eyes may wink, and Romeo
Leap to these arms untalked of and unseen.
Lovers can see to do their amorous rites
By their own beauties; or, if love be blind,
It best agrees with night. Come, civil night,
You sober-suited matron, all in black,
And learn me how to lose a winning match,
Played for a pair of stainless maidenhoods.
Hood my unmanned blood, bating in my cheeks,
With your black mantle till strange love, grown bold,
Think true love acted simple modesty.
Come, night; come, Romeo; come, you day-in-night;
For you will lie upon the wings of night
Whiter than new snow upon a raven's back.
Come, gentle night; come, loving, black-browed night;
Give me my Romeo; and, when he shall die,
Take him and cut him out in little stars,
And he will make the face of heaven so fine
That all the world will be in love with night
And pay no worship to the garish sun.
O, I have bought the mansion of a love,
But not possessed it; and though I am sold,
Not yet enjoyed. So tedious is this day
As is the night before some festival
To an impatient child that has new robes
And may not wear them. O, here comes my nurse,

[*Enter Nurse, with ropes*]

And she brings news; and every tongue that speaks
But Romeo's name speaks heavenly eloquence.
Now, nurse, what news? What have you there? the cords
That Romeo bid you fetch?

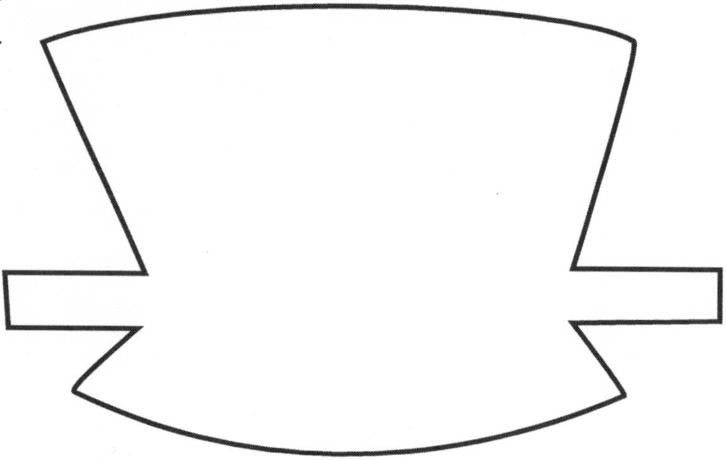

Nurse: Ay, ay, the cords.

[*Throws them down*]

Juliet: Ah me! what news? Why do you wring your hands?

Nurse: Ah, weraday! he's dead, he's dead, he's dead!
We are undone, lady, we are undone!
Alack the day! he's gone, he's killed, he's dead!

Juliet: Can heaven be so envious?

Come, night; come, Romeo; come, you day-in-night

Nurse: Romeo can,
Though heaven cannot. O Romeo, Romeo!
Who ever would have thought it? Romeo!

Juliet: What devil are you that do torment me thus?
This torture should be roared in dismal hell.
Has Romeo slain himself? Say you but "Ay,"
And that bare vowel "Ay" shall poison more
Than the death-darting eye of cockatrice.
I am not I, if there be such an "I";
Or those eyes shut that make you answer "I."
If be be slain, say "I"; or if not, "no."
Brief sounds determine of my weal or woe.

Nurse: I saw the wound, I saw it with my eyes,
(God save the mark!) here on his manly breast.
A piteous corpse, a bloody piteous corpse;
Pale, pale as ashes, all bedaubed in blood,
All in gore-blood. I swooned at the sight.

Juliet: O, break, my heart! poor bankrupt, break at once!
To prison, eyes; never look on liberty!
Vile earth, to earth resign; end motion here,
And you and Romeo press one heavy bier!

Nurse: O Tybalt, Tybalt, the best friend I had!
O courteous Tybalt! honest gentleman
That ever I should live to see you dead!

Juliet: What storm is this that blows so contrary?
Is Romeo slaughtered, and is Tybalt dead?
My dear-loved cousin, and my dearer lord?
Then, dreadful trumpet, sound the general doom!
For who is living, if those two are gone?

Nurse: Tybalt is gone, and Romeo banished;
Romeo that killed him, he is banished.

Juliet: O God! Did Romeo's hand shed Tybalt's blood?

Nurse: It did, it did! Alas the day, it did!

Has Romeo slain himself?

Juliet: O serpent heart, hid with a flowering face!
Did ever dragon keep so fair a cave?
Beautiful tyrant! fiend angelical!
Dove-feathered raven! wolvish-ravening lamb!
Despised substance of divinest show!
Just opposite to what you justly seem—
A damned saint, an honorable villain!
O nature, what had you to do in hell
When you did bower the spirit of a fiend
In mortal paradise of such sweet flesh?
Was ever book containing such vile matter
So fairly bound? O, that deceit should dwell
In such a gorgeous palace!

Nurse: There's no trust,
No faith, no honesty in men; all perjured,
All forsworn, all naught, all dissemblers.
Ah, where's my man? Give me some aqua vitae.
These griefs, these woes, these sorrows make me old.
Shame come to Romeo!

Juliet: Blistered be your tongue
For such a wish! He was not born to shame.
Upon his brow shame is ashamed to sit;
For 'tis a throne where honor may be crowned
Sole monarch of the universal earth.
O, what a beast was I to chide at him!

Nurse: Will you speak well of him that killed your cousin?

Juliet: Shall I speak ill of him that is my husband?
Ah, poor my lord, what tongue shall smooth your name
When I, your three-hours wife, have mangled it?
But wherefore, villain, did you kill my cousin?
That villain cousin would have killed my husband.
Back, foolish tears, back to your native spring!
Your tributary drops belong to woe,
Which you, mistaking, offer up to joy.
My husband lives, that Tybalt would have slain;
And Tybalt's dead, that would have slain my husband.
All this is comfort; wherefore weep I then?

Shall I speak ill of him that is my husband?

Juliet: Some word there was, worser than Tybalt's death,
That murdered me. I would forget it fain;
But O, it presses to my memory
Like damned guilty deeds to sinners' minds!
"Tybalt is dead, and Romeo— banished."
That "banished," that one word "banished,"
Has slain ten thousand Tybalts. Tybalt's death
Was woe enough, if it had ended there;
Or, if sour woe delights in fellowship
And needly will be ranked with other griefs,
Why followed not, when she said "Tybalt's dead,"
Your father, or your mother, nay, or both,
Which modern lamentation might have moved?
But with a rearward following Tybalt's death,
"Romeo is banished"— to speak that word
Is father, mother, Tybalt, Romeo, Juliet,
All slain, all dead. "Romeo is banished"—
There is no end, no limit, measure, bound,
In that word's death; no words can that woe sound.
Where is my father and my mother, nurse?

Nurse: Weeping and wailing over Tybalt's corpse.
Will you go to them? I will bring you there.

Juliet: Wash they his wounds with tears? Mine shall be spent,
When theirs are dry, for Romeo's banishment.
Take up those cords. Poor ropes, you are beguiled,
Both you and I, for Romeo is exiled.
He made you for a highway to my bed;
But I, a maid, die maiden-widowed.
Come, cords; come, Nurse. I'll to my wedding bed;
And death, not Romeo, take my maidenhead!

Nurse: Hie to your chamber. I'll find Romeo
To comfort you. I wot well where he is.
Hark ye, your Romeo will be here at night.
I'll to him; he is hid at Laurence's cell.

Juliet: O, find him! give this ring to my true knight
And bid him come to take his last farewell.

[*Exit*]

3

[*Friar Laurence's cell*]

[*Enter Friar Laurence*]

Friar Laurence: Romeo, come forth; come forth, you fearful man.
Affliction is enamoured of your parts,
And you are wedded to calamity.

[*Enter Romeo*]

Romeo: Father, what news? What is the Prince's doom
What sorrow craves acquaintance at my hand
That I yet know not?

Friar Laurence: Too familiar
Is my dear son with such sour company.
I bring you tidings of the Prince's doom.

Romeo: What less than doomsday is the Prince's doom?

Friar Laurence: A gentler judgment vanished from his lips—
Not body's death, but body's banishment.

Romeo: Ha, banishment? Be merciful, say "death";
For exile has more terror in his look,
Much more than death. Do not say "banishment."

Friar Laurence: Hence from Verona are you banished.
Be patient, for the world is broad and wide.

Romeo: There is no world without Verona walls,
But purgatory, torture, hell itself.
Banished from here is banished from the world,
And world's exile is death. Then "banishment"
Is death mistermed. Calling death "banishment,"
You cut my head off with a golden axe
And smile upon the stroke that murders me.

Friar Laurence: O deadly sin! O rude unthankfulness!
Your fault our law calls death; but the kind Prince,
Taking your part, has brushed aside the law,
And turned that black word "death" to banishment.
This is dear mercy, and you see it not.

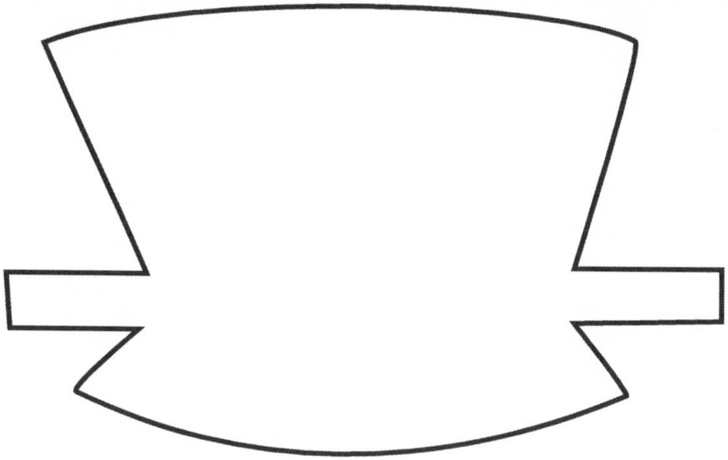

Romeo: 'Tis torture, and not mercy. Heaven is here,
Where Juliet lives; and every cat and dog
And little mouse, every unworthy thing,
Live here in heaven and may look on her;
But Romeo may not. More validity,
More honorable state, more courtship lives
In carrion flies than Romeo. They may seize
On the white wonder of dear Juliet's hand
And steal immortal blessing from her lips,
Who, even in pure and vestal modesty,
Still blush, as thinking their own kisses sin;
But Romeo may not— he is banished.
This may flies do, when I from this must fly;
They are free men, but I am banished.
And say you yet that exile is not death?
Had you no poison mixed, no sharp-ground knife,
No sudden mean of death, though never so mean,
But "banished" to kill me— "banished"?
O friar, the damned use that word in hell;
Howling attends it! How have you the heart,
Being a divine, a ghostly confessor,
A sin-absolver, and my friend professed,
To mangle me with that word "banished"?

Friar Laurence: You fond mad man, hear me a little speak.

Romeo: O, you will speak again of banishment.

Friar Laurence: I'll give you armor to keep off that word;
Adversity's sweet milk, philosophy,
To comfort you, though you are banished.

Romeo: Yet "banished"? Hang up philosophy!
Unless philosophy can make a Juliet,
Displant a town, reverse a prince's doom,
It helps not, it prevails not. Talk no more.

Friar Laurence: O, then I see that madmen have no ears.

Romeo: How should they, when that wise men have no eyes?

Friar Laurence: Let me dispute with you of your estate.

Romeo: You cannot speak of that you do not feel.
Were you as young as I, Juliet your love,
An hour but married, Tybalt murdered,
Doting like me, and like me banished,
Then might you speak, then might you tear your hair,
And fall upon the ground, as I do now,
Taking the measure of an unmade grave.

O, then I see that madmen have no ears.

[*Knock within*]

Friar Laurence: Arise; one knocks. Good Romeo, hide yourself.

Romeo: Not I; unless the breath of heartsick groans,
Mist-like infold me from the search of eyes.

[*Knock*]

Friar Laurence: Hark, how they knock! Who's there? Romeo, arise;
You will be taken.— Stay awhile!— Stand up;

[*Knock*]

Run to my study.— By-and-by!— God's will,
What simpleness is this.— I come, I come!

[*Knock*]

Who knocks so hard? Whence come you? What's your will?

Nurse: [*within*] Let me come in, and you shall know my errand.
I come from Lady Juliet.

Friar Laurence: Welcome then.

[*Enter Nurse*]

Nurse: O holy friar, O, tell me, holy friar
Where is my lady's lord, where's Romeo?

Friar Laurence: There on the ground, with his own tears made drunk.

Nurse: O, he is even in my mistress' case,
Just in her case!

Friar Laurence: O woeful sympathy!
Piteous predicament!

Nurse: Even so lies she,
Blubbering and weeping, weeping and blubbering.
Stand up, stand up! Stand, if you be a man.
For Juliet's sake, for her sake, rise and stand!
Why should you fall into so deep an O?

Romeo: [*rises*] Nurse—

Nurse: Ah sir! ah sir! Well, death's the end of all.

Romeo: Spoke you of Juliet? How is it with her?
Does not she think me an old murderer,
Now I have stained the childhood of our joy
With blood removed but little from her own?
Where is she? and how does she! and what says
My concealed lady to our cancelled love?

Nurse: O, she says nothing, sir, but weeps and weeps;
And now falls on her bed, and then starts up,
And Tybalt calls; and then on Romeo cries,
And then down falls again.

Romeo: As if that name,
Shot from the deadly level of a gun,
Did murder her; as that name's cursed hand
Murdered her kinsman. O, tell me, friar, tell me,
In what vile part of this anatomy
Does my name lodge? Tell me, that I may sack
The hateful mansion.

[*Draws his dagger*]

Does not she think me an old murderer

Friar Laurence: Hold your desperate hand.
Are you a man? your form cries out you are;
Your tears are womanish, your wild acts denote
The unreasonable fury of a beast.
Unseemly woman in a seeming man!
Or ill-beseeming beast in seeming both!
You have amazed me. By my holy order,
I thought your disposition better tempered.
Have you slain Tybalt? Will you slay yourself?
And slay your lady that in your life lives,
By doing damned hate upon yourself?
Why rail you on your birth, the heaven, and earth?
Since birth and heaven and earth, all three do meet
In you at once; which you at once would lose.
Fie, fie, you shame your shape, your love, your wit,
Which, like a usurer, abound in all,
And use none in that true use indeed
Which should bedeck your shape, your love, your wit.
Your noble shape is but a form of wax
Digressing from the valor of a man;
Your dear love sworn but hollow perjury,
Killing that love which you have vowed to cherish;
Your wit, that ornament to shape and love,
Misshapen in the conduct of them both,
Like powder in a skill-less soldier's flask,
Is get afire by your own ignorance,
And you dismembered with your own defense.
What, rouse you, man! your Juliet is alive,
For whose dear sake you were but lately dead.
There are you happy. Tybalt would kill you,
But you slew Tybalt. There are you happy too.
The law, that threatened death, becomes your friend
And turns it to exile. There are you happy.
A pack of blessings light upon your back;
Happiness courts you in her best array;
But, like a misbehaved and sullen wench,
You pout upon your fortune and your love.
Take heed, take heed, for such die miserable.
Go get you to your love, as was decreed,
Ascend her chamber, hence and comfort her.
But look you stay not till the watch be set,
For then you can not pass to Mantua,
Where you shall live till we can find a time
To blaze your marriage, reconcile your friends,
Beg pardon of the Prince, and call you back
With twenty hundred thousand times more joy
Than you went forth in lamentation.
Go before, Nurse. Commend me to your lady,
And bid her hasten all the house to bed,
Which heavy sorrow makes them apt unto.
Romeo is coming.

Nurse: O Lord, I could have stayed here all the night
To hear good counsel. O, what learning is!
My lord, I'll tell my lady you will come.

Romeo: Do so, and bid my sweet prepare to chide.

Nurse: Here is a ring she bid me give you, sir.
Hie you, make haste, for it grows very late.

[*Exit*]

Romeo: How well my comfort is revived by this!

Friar Laurence: Go forth; good night; and here stands all your state:
Either be gone before the watch be set,
Or by the break of day disguised from here.
Sojourn in Mantua. I'll find out your man,
And he shall signify from time to time
Every good hap to you that chances here.
Give me your hand. 'tis late. Farewell; good night.

Romeo: But that a joy past joy calls out on me,
It were a grief so brief to part with you.
Farewell.

[*Exit*]

Sojourn in Mantua. I'll find out your man

4

[Capulet's house]

[Enter Capulet, Lady Capulet, and Paris]

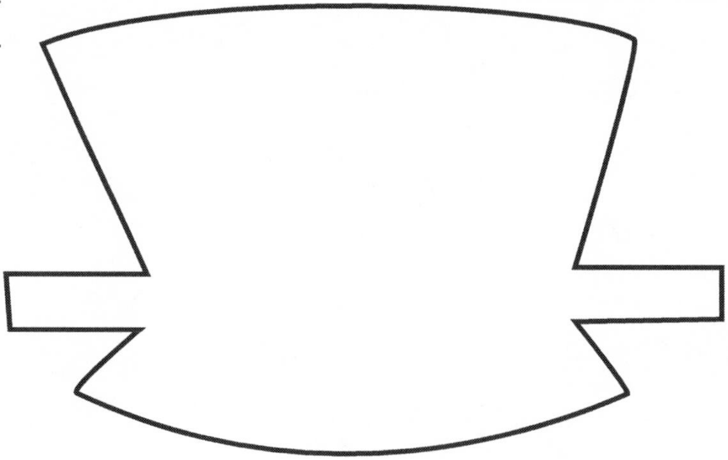

Capulet: Things have fallen out, sir, so unluckily
That we have had no time to move our daughter.
Look you, she loved her kinsman Tybalt dearly,
And so did I. Well, we were born to die.
'Tis very late; she'll not come down tonight.
I promise you, but for your company,
I would have been abed an hour ago.

Paris: These times of woe afford no tune to woo.
Madam, good night. Commend me to your daughter.
Lady. I will, and know her mind early tomorrow;
Tonight she's mewed up to her heaviness.

Capulet: Sir Paris, I will make a desperate tender
Of my child's love. I think she will be ruled
In all respects by me; nay more, I doubt it not.
Wife, go you to her before you go to bed;
Acquaint her here of my son Paris' love
And bid her (mark you me?) on Wednesday next—
But, soft! what day is this?

Paris: Monday, my lord.

Capulet: Monday! ha, ha! Well, Wednesday is too soon.
Thursday let it be— a Thursday, tell her
She shall be married to this noble earl.
Will you be ready? Do you like this haste?
We'll keep no great ado— a friend or two;
For hark you, Tybalt being slain so late,
It may be thought we held him carelessly,
Being our kinsman, if we revel much.
Therefore we'll have some half a dozen friends,
And there an end. But what say you to Thursday?

Paris: My lord, I would that Thursday were tomorrow.

Capulet: Well, get you gone. A Thursday be it then.
Go you to Juliet before you go to bed;
Prepare her, wife, against this wedding day.
Farewell, My lord.— Light to my chamber, ho!
Afore me, It is so very very late
That we may call it early by-and-by.
Good night.

[Exit]

Thursday, tell her
She shall be married to this noble earl.

5

[Capulet's orchard]

[Enter Romeo and Juliet aloft, at the Window]

Juliet: Will you be gone? It is not yet near day.
It was the nightingale, and not the lark,
That pierced the fearful hollow of your ear.
Nightly she sings on yond pomegranate tree.
Believe me, love, it was the nightingale.

Romeo: It was the lark, the herald of the morn;
No nightingale. Look, love, what envious streaks
Do lace the severing clouds in yonder East.
Night's candles are burnt out, and jocund day
Stands tiptoe on the misty mountain tops.
I must be gone and live, or stay and die.

Juliet: Yond light is not daylight; I know it, I.
It is some meteor that the sun exhales
To be to you this night a torchbearer
And light you on the way to Mantua.
Therefore stay yet; you need not to be gone.

Romeo: Let me be taken, let me be put to death.
I am content, so you will have it so.
I'll say yon gray is not the morning's eye,
'Tis but the pale reflex of Cynthia's brow;
Nor that is not the lark whose notes do beat
The vaulty heaven so high above our heads.
I have more care to stay than will to go.
Come, death, and welcome! Juliet wills it so.
How is it, my soul? Let's talk; it is not day.

Juliet: It is, it is! Hurry now, be gone, away!
It is the lark that sings so out of tune,
Straining harsh discords and unpleasing sharps.
Some say the lark makes sweet division;
This does not so, for she divides us.
Some say the lark and loathed toad changed eyes;
O, now I would they had changed voices too,
Since arm from arm that voice does us affray,
Hunting you away with hunt's-up to the day!
O, now be gone! More light and light it grows.

Romeo: More light and light— more dark and dark our woes!

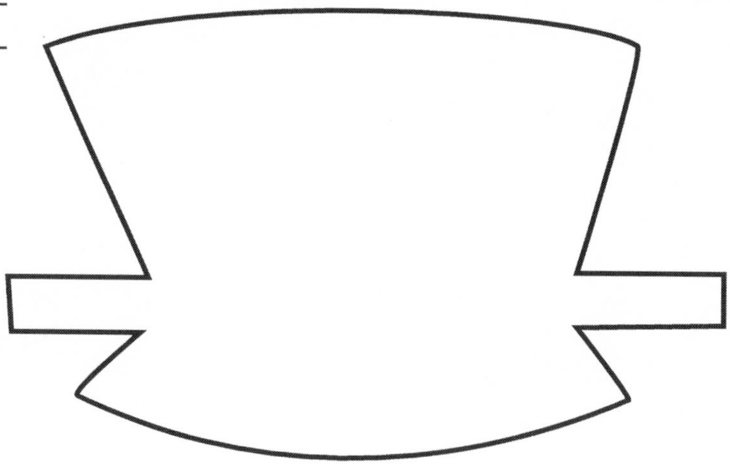

[*Enter Nurse*]

Nurse: Madam!

Juliet: Nurse?

Nurse: Your lady mother is coming to your chamber.
The day is broke; be wary, look about.

[*Exit*]

Juliet: Then, window, let day in, and let life out.

Romeo: Farewell, farewell! One kiss, and I'll descend.

[*He goes down*]

Juliet: Are you gone so, my lord, my love, my friend?
I must hear from you every day in the hour,
For in a minute there are many days.
O, by this count I shall be much in years
Before I again behold my Romeo!

Romeo: Farewell!
I will omit no opportunity
That may convey my greetings, love, to you.

Juliet: O, think you we shall ever meet again?

Romeo: I doubt it not; and all these woes shall serve
For sweet discourses in our time to come.

Juliet: O God, I have an ill-divining soul!
I think I see you, now you are below,
As one dead in the bottom of a tomb.
Either my eyesight fails, or you look pale.

Romeo: And trust me, love, in my eye so do you.
Dry sorrow drinks our blood. Adieu, adieu!

[*Exit*]

Juliet: O Fortune, Fortune! all men call you fickle.
If you are fickle, what do you with him
That is renowned for faith? Be fickle, Fortune,
For then I hope you will not keep him long
But send him back.

O Fortune, Fortune! all men call you fickle.

Lady Capulet: [*within*] Ho, daughter! are you up?

Juliet: Who is it that calls? It is my lady mother.
Is she not down so late, or up so early?
What unaccustomed cause procures her here?

[*Enter Mother*]

Lady Capulet: Why, how now, Juliet?

Juliet: Madam, I am not well.

Lady Capulet: Evermore weeping for your cousin's death?
What, will you wash him from his grave with tears?
But if you could, you could not make him live.
Therefore have done. Some grief shows much of love;
But much of grief shows still some want of wit.

Juliet: Yet let me weep for such a feeling loss.

Lady Capulet: So shall you feel the loss, but not the friend
Which you weep for.

Juliet: Feeling so the loss,
I cannot choose but ever weep the friend.

Lady Capulet: Well, girl, you weep not so much for his death
As that the villain lives which slaughtered him.

Juliet: What villain, madam?

Lady Capulet: That same villain Romeo.

Juliet: [*aside*] Villain and he be many miles asunder.—
God pardon him! I do, with all my heart;
And yet no man like he does grieve my heart.

Lady Capulet: That is because the traitor murderer lives.

Juliet:Yes, madam, from the reach of these my hands.
Would none but I might avenge my cousin's death!

Lady Capulet: We will have vengeance for it, fear you not.
Then weep no more. I'll send to one in Mantua,
Where that same banished runagate does live,
Shall give him such an unaccustomed dram
That he shall soon keep Tybalt company;
And then I hope you will be satisfied.

Juliet: Indeed I never shall be satisfied
With Romeo till I behold him— dead—
Is my poor heart so for a kinsman vexed.
Madam, if you could find out but a man
To bear a poison, I would temper it;
That Romeo should, upon receipt thereof,
Soon sleep in quiet. O, how my heart abhors
To hear him named and cannot come to him,
To wreak the love I bore my cousin Tybalt
Upon his body that has slaughtered him!

Lady Capulet: Find you the means, and I'll find such a man.

Indeed I never shall be satisfied
With Romeo till I behold him

Lady Capulet: But now I'll tell you joyful tidings, girl.

Juliet: And joy comes well in such a needy time.
What are they, I beseech your ladyship?

Lady Capulet: Well, well, you have a careful father, child;
One who, to put you from your heaviness,
Has sorted out a sudden day of joy
That you expect not nor I looked not for.

Juliet: Madam, in happy time! What day is that?

Lady Capulet: Indeed, my child, early next Thursday morn
The gallant, young, and noble gentleman,
The Count Paris, at Saint Peter's Church,
Shall happily make you there a joyful bride.

Juliet: Now by Saint Peter's Church, and Peter too,
He shall not make me there a joyful bride!
I wonder at this haste, that I must wed
Before he that should be husband comes to woo.
I pray you tell my lord and father, madam,
I will not marry yet; and when I do, I swear
It shall be Romeo, whom you know I hate,
Rather than Paris. These are news indeed!

Lady Capulet: Here comes your father. Tell him so yourself,
And see how be will take it at your hands.

He shall not make me there a joyful bride!

[*Enter Capulet and Nurse*]

Capulet: When the sun sets the air does drizzle dew,
But for the sunset of my brother's son
It rains downright.
How now? a conduit, girl? What, still in tears?
Evermore showering? In one little body
You counterfeit a bark, a sea, a wind—
For still your eyes, which I may call the sea,
Do ebb and flow with tears; the bark your body is
Sailing in this salt flood; the winds, your sighs,
Who, raging with your tears and they with them,
Without a sudden calm will overset
Your tempest-tossed body. How now, wife?
Have you delivered to her our decree?

Lady Capulet:Yes, sir; but she will none, she gives you thanks.
I would the fool were married to her grave!

Capulet: Soft! take me with you, take me with you, wife.
How? Will she none? Does she not give us thanks?
Is she not proud? Does she not count her blessed,
Unworthy as she is, that we have wrought
So worthy a gentleman to be her bridegroom?

Juliet: Not proud you have, but thankful that you have.
Proud can I never be of what I hate,
But thankful even for hate that is meant love.

Capulet: How, how, how, how, choplogic? What is this?
"Proud"— and "I thank you"— and "I thank you not"—
And yet "not proud"? Mistress minion you,
Thank me no thankings, nor proud me no prouds,
But fettle your fine joints against Thursday next
To go with Paris to Saint Peter's Church,
Or I will drag you on a sledge there.
Out, you green-sickness carrion I out, you baggage!
You tallow-face!

Lady Capulet: Fie, fie! what, are you mad?

Juliet: Good father, I beseech you on my knees,
Hear me with patience but to speak a word.

Capulet: Hang you, young baggage! disobedient wretch!
I tell you what— get you to church a Thursday
Or never after look me in the face.
Speak not, reply not, do not answer me!
My fingers itch. Wife, we scarce thought us blessed
That God had lent us but this only child;
But now I see this one is one too much,
And that we have a curse in having her.
Out on her, wretch!

How, how, how, how, choplogic? What is this?
"Proud"— and "I thank you"— and "I thank you not"

Nurse: God in heaven bless her!
You are to blame, my lord, to rate her so.

Capulet: And why, my Lady Wisdom? Hold your tongue,
Good Prudence. Smatter with your gossips, go!

Nurse: I speak no treason.

Capulet: O, God in heaven!

Nurse: May not one speak?

Capulet: Peace, you mumbling fool!
Utter your gravity over a gossip's bowl,
For here we need it not.

Lady Capulet: You are too hot.

Capulet: God's bread it makes me mad. Day, night, late, early,
At home, abroad, alone, in company,
Waking or sleeping, still my care has been
To have her matched; and having now provided
A gentleman of princely parentage,
Of fair demesnes, youthful, and nobly trained,
Stuffed, as they say, with honorable parts,
Proportioned as one's thought would wish a man—
And then to have a wretched puling fool,
A whining mammet, in her fortune's tender,
To answer "I'll not wed, I cannot love;
I am too young, I pray you pardon me"!
But, if you will not wed, I'll pardon you.
Graze where you will, you shall not house with me.
Look to it, think on it; I do not use to jest.
Thursday is near; lay hand on heart, advise:
If you be mine, I'll give you to my friend;
If you be not, hang, beg, starve, die in the streets,
For, by my soul, I'll never acknowledge you,
Nor what is mine shall never do you good.
Trust to it. Bethink you. I'll not be forsworn.

[*Exit*]

Juliet: Is there no pity sitting in the clouds
That sees into the bottom of my grief?
O sweet my mother, cast me not away!
Delay this marriage for a month, a week;
Or if you do not, make the bridal bed
In that dim monument where Tybalt lies.

Lady Capulet: Talk not to me, for I'll not speak a word.
Do as you will, for I have done with you.

[*Exit*]

But, if you will not wed, I'll pardon you. Graze where you will, you shall not house with me.

Juliet: O God!— O nurse, how shall this be prevented?
My husband is on earth, my faith in heaven.
How shall that faith return again to earth
Unless that husband send it me from heaven
By leaving earth? Comfort me, counsel me.
Alack, alack, that heaven should practice stratagems
Upon so soft a subject as myself!
What say you? Have you not a word of joy?
Some comfort, nurse.

Nurse: Faith, here it is.
Romeo is banished; and all the world to nothing
That he dares never come back to challenge you;
Or if he do, it needs must be by stealth.
Then, since the case so stands as now it does,
I think it best you married with the Count.
O, he's a lovely gentleman!
Romeo's a dishclout to him. An eagle, madam,
Has not so green, so quick, so fair an eye
As Paris has. Beshrew my very heart,
I think you are happy in this second match,
For it excels your first; or if it did not,
Your first is dead— or 'twere as good he were
As living here and you no use of him.

Juliet: Speak you this from your heart?

Nurse: And from my soul too; else beshrew them both.

Juliet: Amen!

Nurse: What?

Juliet: Well, you have comforted me marvellous much.
Go in; and tell my lady I am gone,
Having displeased my father, to Laurence's cell,
To make confession and to be absolved.

Nurse: Surely, I will; and this is wisely done.

[*Exit*]

Juliet: Ancient damnation! O most wicked fiend!
Is it more sin to wish me thus forsworn,
Or to dispraise my lord with that same tongue
Which she has praised him with above compare
So many thousand times? Go, counsellor!
You and my bosom henceforth shall be twain.
I'll to the friar to know his remedy.
If all else fail, myself have power to die.

[*Exit*]

I think it best you married with the Count. O, he's a lovely gentleman!

Act Four

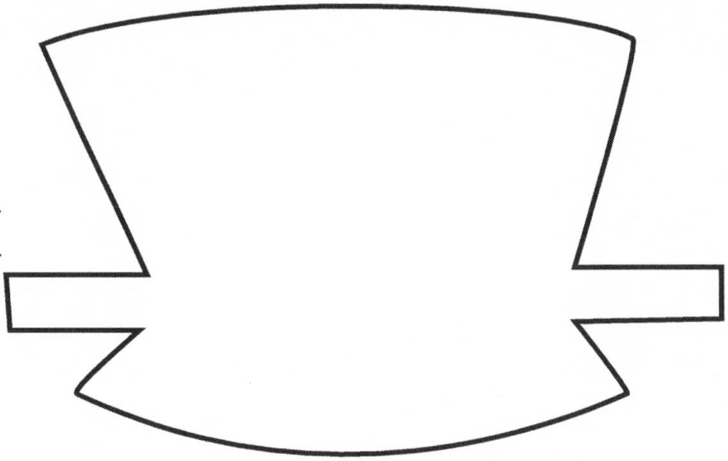

1

[Friar Laurence's cell]

[Enter Friar Laurence and Count Paris]

Friar Laurence: On Thursday, sir? The time is very short.

Paris: My father Capulet will have it so,
And I am nothing slow to slack his haste.

Friar Laurence: You say you do not know the lady's mind.
Uneven is the course; I like it not.

Paris: Immoderately she weeps for Tybalt's death,
And therefore have I little talked of love;
For Venus smiles not in a house of tears.
Now, sir, her father counts it dangerous
That she do give her sorrow so much sway,
And in his wisdom hastes our marriage
To stop the inundation of her tears,
Which, too much minded by herself alone,
May be put from her by society.
Now do you know the reason of this haste.

Friar Laurence: [*aside*] I wish I knew not why it should be slowed.—
Look, sir, here comes the lady toward my cell.

in his wisdom hastes our marriage
To stop the inundation of her tears

[*Enter Juliet*]

Paris: Happily met, my lady and my wife!

Juliet: That may be, sir, when I may be a wife.

Paris: That may be must be, love, on Thursday next.

Juliet: What must be shall be.

Friar Laurence: That's a certain text.

Paris: Come you to make confession to this father?

Juliet: To answer that, I should confess to you.

Paris: Do not deny to him that you love me.

Juliet: I will confess to you that I love him.

Paris: So will you, I am sure, that you love me.

Juliet: If I do so, it will be of more price,
Being spoke behind your back, than to your face.

Paris: Poor soul, your face is much abused with tears.

Juliet: The tears have got small victory by that,
For it was bad enough before their spite.

Paris: You wrong it more than tears with that report.

Juliet: That is no slander, sir, which is a truth;
And what I spoke, I spoke it to my face.

Paris: Your face is mine, and you have slandered it.

Juliet: It may be so, for it is not my own.
Are you at leisure, holy father, now,
Or shall I come to you at evening mass?

Friar: My leisure serves me, pensive daughter, now.
My lord, we must entreat the time alone.

Paris: God shield I should disturb devotion!
Juliet, on Thursday early will I rouse you.
Till then, adieu, and keep this holy kiss.

[*Exit*]

Are you at leisure, holy father, now,
Or shall I come to you at evening mass?

Juliet: O, shut the door! and when you have done so,
Come weep with me— past hope, past cure, past help!

Friar Laurence: Ah, Juliet, I already know your grief;
It strains me past the compass of my wits.
I hear you must, and nothing may delay it,
On Thursday next be married to this Count.

Juliet: Tell me not, friar, that you hear of this,
Unless you tell me how I may prevent it.
If in your wisdom you can give no help,
Do you but call my resolution wise
And with this knife I'll help it presently.
God joined my heart and Romeo's, you our hands;
And before this hand, by you to Romeo's sealed,
Shall be the label to another deed,
Or my true heart with treacherous revolt
Turn to another, this shall slay them both.
Therefore, out of your long-experienced time,
Give me some present counsel; or, behold,
'Twixt my extremes and me, this bloody knife
Shall play the umpire, arbitrating that
Which the commission of your years and art
Could to no issue of true honor bring.
Be not so long to speak. I long to die
If what you speak speak not of remedy.

Friar Laurence: Hold, daughter. I do espy a kind of hope,
Which craves as desperate an execution
As that is desperate which we would prevent.
If, rather than to marry Count Paris
You have the strength of will to slay yourself,
Then is it likely you will undertake
A thing like death to chide away this shame,
That cope with death himself to escape from it;
And, if you dare, I'll give you remedy.

Juliet: O, bid me leap, rather than marry Paris,
From off the battlements of yonder tower,
Or walk in thievish ways, or bid me lurk
Where serpents are; chain me with roaring bears,
Or shut me nightly in a charnel house,
Overcovered quite with dead men's rattling bones,
With reeky shanks and yellow chapless skulls;
Or bid me go into a new-made grave
And hide me with a dead man in his shroud—
Things that, to hear them told, have made me tremble—
And I will do it without fear or doubt,
To live an unstained wife to my sweet love.

God joined my heart and Romeo's, you our hands

Friar Laurence: Hold, then. Go home, be merry, give consent
To marry Paris. Wednesday is tomorrow.
Tomorrow night look that you lie alone;
Let not the nurse lie with you in your chamber.
Take you this vial, being then in bed,
And this distilled liquor drink you off;
When presently through all your veins shall run
A cold and drowsy humor; for no pulse
Shall keep his native progress, but surcease;
No warmth, no breath, shall testify you live;
The roses in your lips and cheeks shall fade
To pale ashes, your eyes' windows fall
Like death when he shuts up the day of life;
Each part, deprived of supple government,
Shall, stiff and stark and cold, appear like death;
And in this borrowed likeness of shrunk death
You shall continue two-and-forty hours,
And then awake as from a pleasant sleep.
Now, when the bridegroom in the morning comes
To rouse you from your bed, there are you dead.
Then, as the manner of our country is,
In your best robes uncovered on the bier
You shall be borne to that same ancient vault
Where all the kindred of the Capulets lie.
In the mean time, against you shall awake,
Shall Romeo by my letters know our drift;
And here shall he come; and he and I
Will watch your waking, and that very night
Shall Romeo bear you hence to Mantua.
And this shall free you from this present shame,
If no inconstant toy nor womanish fear
Abate your valor in the acting it.

Juliet: Give me, give me! O, tell not me of fear!

Friar Laurence: Hold! Get you gone, be strong and prosperous
In this resolve. I'll send a friar with speed
To Mantua, with my letters to your lord.

Juliet: Love give me strength! and strength shall help afford.
Farewell, dear father.

[*Exit*]

through all your veins shall run a cold and drowsy humor

2

[*Capulet's house*]

[*Enter Capulet, Lady Capulet, Nurse, and Servants*]

Capulet: So many guests invite as here are writ.

[*Exit a Servant*]

Sirrah, go hire me twenty cunning cooks.

Servant: You shall have none ill, sir; for I'll try if they can lick their fingers.

Capulet: How can you try them so?

Servant: Well, sir, 'tis an ill cook that cannot lick his own fingers. Therefore he that cannot lick his fingers goes not with me.

Capulet: Go, begone.

[*Exit Servant*]

We shall be much unfurnished for this time.
What, is my daughter gone to Friar Laurence?

Nurse: Ay, forsooth.

Capulet: Well, be may chance to do some good on her.
A peevish self-willed harlotry it is.

[*Enter Juliet*]

Nurse: See where she comes from shrift with merry look.

Capulet: How now, my headstrong? Where have you been gadding?

Juliet: Where I have learnt me to repent the sin
Of disobedient opposition
To you and your behests, and am enjoined
By holy Laurence to fall prostrate here
To beg your pardon. Pardon, I beseech you!
Henceforward I am ever ruled by you.

Capulet: Send for the Count. Go tell him of this.
I'll have this knot knit up tomorrow morning.

Juliet: I met the youthful lord at Laurence's cell
And gave him what becomed love I might,
Not stepping over the bounds of modesty.

Capulet: Why, I am glad of it. This is well. Stand up.
This is as it should be. Let me see the Count.

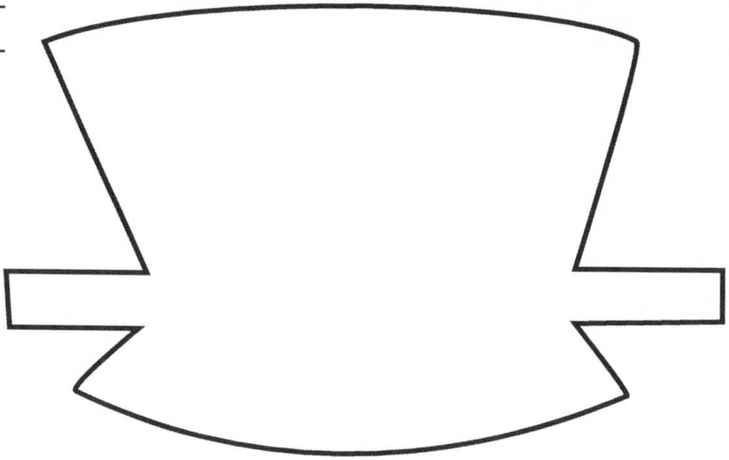

Ay, well, go, I say, and fetch him here.
Now, afore God, this reverend holy friar,
All our whole city is much bound to him.

I have learnt me to repent the sin of disobedient opposition

Juliet: Nurse, will you go with me into my closet
To help me sort such needful ornaments
As you think fit to furnish me tomorrow?

Lady Capulet: No, not till Thursday. There is time enough.

Capulet: Go, nurse, go with her. We'll to church tomorrow.

[*Exit Juliet and Nurse*]

Lady Capulet: We shall be short in our provision.
'Tis now near night.

Capulet: Tush, I will stir about,
And all things shall be well, I warrant you, wife.
Go you to Juliet, help to deck up her.
I'll not to bed tonight; let me alone.
I'll play the housewife for this once. What, ho!
They are all forth; well, I will walk myself
To Count Paris, to prepare him up
Against tomorrow. My heart is wondrous light,
Since this same wayward girl is so reclaimed.

[*Exit*]

My heart is wondrous light,
Since this same wayward girl is so reclaimed.

3

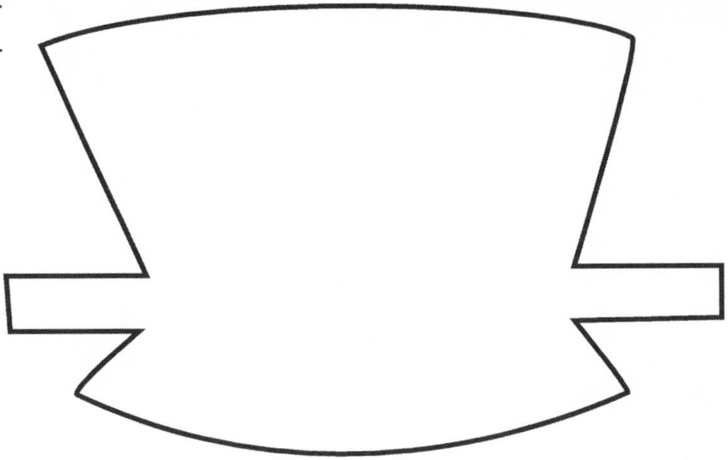

[*Juliet's chamber*]

[*Enter Juliet and Nurse*]

Juliet: Yes, those attires are best; but, gentle nurse,
I pray you leave me to myself tonight;
For I have need of many orisons
To move the heavens to smile upon my state,
Which, well you know, is cross and full of sin.

[*Enter Lady Capulet*]

Lady Capulet: What, are you busy, ho? Need you my help?

Juliet: No, madam; we have culled such necessaries
As are behooved for our state tomorrow.
So please you, let me now be left alone,
And let the nurse this night sit up with you;
For I am sure you have your hands full all
In this so sudden business.

Lady Capulet: Good night.
Get you to bed, and rest; for you have need.

[*Exit Mother and Nurse*]

Juliet: Farewell! God knows when we shall meet again.
I have a faint cold fear thrills through my veins
That almost freezes up the heat of life.
I'll call them back again to comfort me.
Nurse!— What should she do here?
My dismal scene I needs must act alone.
Come, vial.
What if this mixture do not work at all?
Shall I be married then tomorrow morning?
No, No! This shall forbid it. Lie you there.

[*Lays down a dagger*]

My dismal scene I needs must act alone.

Juliet: What if it be a poison which the friar
Subtlely has ministered to have me dead,
Lest in this marriage he should be dishonored
Because he married me before to Romeo?
I fear it is; and yet I think it should not,
For he has still been tried a holy man.
I will not entertain so bad a thought.
How if, when I am laid into the tomb,
I wake before the time that Romeo
Come to redeem me? There's a fearful point!
Shall I not then be stifled in the vault,
To whose foul mouth no healthsome air breathes in,
And there die strangled before my Romeo comes?
Or, if I live, is it not very like
The horrible conceit of death and night,
Together with the terror of the place—
As in a vault, an ancient receptacle
Where for this many hundred years the bones
Of all my buried ancestors are packed;
Where bloody Tybalt, yet but green in earth,
Lies festering in his shroud; where, as they say,
At some hours in the night spirits resort—
Alack, alack, is it not like that I,
So early waking— what with loathsome smells,
And shrieks like mandrakes torn out of the earth,
That living mortals, hearing them, run mad—
O, if I wake, shall I not be distraught,
Environed with all these hideous fears,
And madly play with my forefathers' joints,
And pluck the mangled Tybalt from his shroud.,
And, in this rage, with some great kinsman's bone
As with a club dash out my desperate brains?
O, look! I think I see my cousin's ghost
Seeking out Romeo, that did spit his body
Upon a rapier's point. Stay, Tybalt, stay!
Romeo, I come! this do I drink to you.

[*She drinks and falls*]

Romeo, I come! this do I drink to you.

4

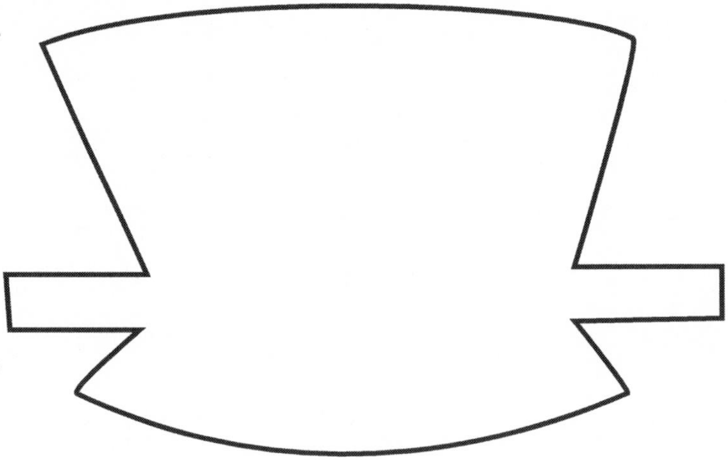

[Capulet's house]

[Enter Lady Capulet and Nurse]

Lady Capulet: Hold, take these keys and fetch more spices, Nurse.

Nurse: They call for dates and quinces in the pastry.

[Enter Old Capulet]

Capulet: Come, stir, stir, stir! The second cock has crowed,
The curfew bell has rung, 'tis three o'clock.
Look to the baked meats, good Angelica;
Spare not for cost.

Nurse: Go, you cot-quean, go,
Get you to bed! Faith, you'll be sick tomorrow
For this night's watching.

Capulet: No, not a whit. What, I have watched before now
All night for lesser cause, and never been sick.

Lady Capulet:Yes, you have been a mouse-hunt in your time;
But I will watch you from such watching now.

[Exit Lady and Nurse]

Capulet: A jealous hood, a jealous hood!

[Enter several fellows, with spits, logs, baskets]

What is there? Now, fellow,

Fellow: Things for the cook, sir; but I know not what.

Capulet: Make haste, make haste.

[Exit First Fellow]

Sirrah, fetch drier logs.
Call Peter; he will show you where they are.

Fellow: I have a head, sir, that will find out logs
And never trouble Peter for the matter.

Capulet: Mass, and well said; a merry whoreson, ha!
You shall be loggerhead.

[Exit Fellow]

Good faith, 'tis day.
The Count will be here with music straight,
For so he said he would.

[Play music]

I hear him near.
Nurse! Wife! What, ho! What, nurse, I say!

[Enter Nurse]

Go waken Juliet; go and trim her up.
I'll go and chat with Paris. Hie, make haste,
Make haste! The bridegroom he is come already:
Make haste, I say.

[Exit]

Go waken Juliet; go and trim her up.

5

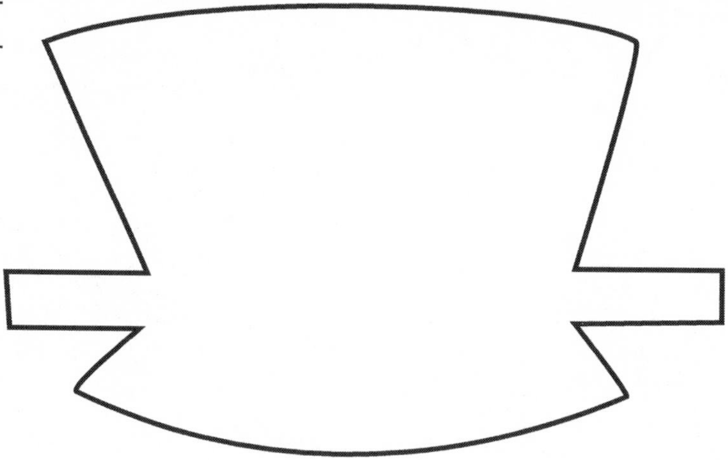

[*Juliet's chamber*]

[*Enter Nurse*]

Nurse: Mistress! what, mistress! Juliet! Fast, I warrant her, she.
Why, lamb! why, lady! Fie, you slug-abed!
Why, love, I say! madam! sweetheart! Why, bride!
What, not a word? You take your pennyworths now!
Sleep for a week; for the next night, I warrant,
The Count Paris has set up his rest
That you shall rest but little. God forgive me!
Well, and amen. How sound is she asleep!
I needs must wake her. Madam, madam, madam!
Ay, let the Count take you in your bed!
He'll fright you up, in faith. Will it not be?

[*Draws aside the curtains*]

What, dressed, and in your clothes, and down again?
I must needs wake you. Lady! lady! lady!
Alas, alas! Help, help! My lady's dead!
O weraday that ever I was born!
Some aqua-vitae, ho! My lord! my lady!

[*Enter Lady Capulet*]

Lady Capulet: What noise is here?

Nurse: O lamentable day!

Lady Capulet: What is the matter?

Nurse: Look, look! O heavy day!

Lady Capulet: O me, O me! My child, my only life!
Revive, look up, or I will die with you!
Help, help! Call help.

Alas, alas! Help, help! My lady's dead!

[*Enter Capulet*]

Capulet: For shame, bring Juliet forth; her lord is come.

Nurse: She's dead, deceased; she's dead! Alack the day!

Lady Capulet: Alack the day, she's dead, she's dead, she's dead!

Capulet: Ha! let me see her. Out alas! she's cold,
Her blood is settled, and her joints are stiff;
Life and these lips have long been separated.
Death lies on her like an untimely frost
Upon the sweetest flower of all the field.

Nurse: O lamentable day!

Lady Capulet: O woeful time!

Capulet: Death, that has taken her away to make me wail,
Ties up my tongue and will not let me speak.

[*Enter Friar Laurence, Count Paris, Musicians*]

Friar Laurence: Come, is the bride ready to go to church?

Capulet: Ready to go, but never to return.
O son, the night before your wedding day
Has Death lain with your wife. See, there she lies,
Flower as she was, deflowered by him.
Death is my son-in-law, Death is my heir;
My daughter he has wedded. I will die
And leave him all. Life, living, all is Death's.

Paris: Have I thought long to see this morning's face,
And does it give me such a sight as this?
Mother. Accursed, unhappy, wretched, hateful day!
Most miserable hour that ever time saw
In lasting labour of his pilgrimage!
But one, poor one, one poor and loving child,
But one thing to rejoice and solace in,
And cruel Death has catched it from my sight!

Nurse: O woe? O woeful, woeful, woeful day!
Most lamentable day, most woeful day
That ever ever I did yet behold!
O day! O day! O day! O hateful day!
Never was seen so black a day as this.
O woeful day! O woeful day!

Paris: Beguiled, divorced, wronged, spited, slain!
Most detestable Death, by you beguiled,
By cruel cruel you quite overthrown!
O love! O life! not life, but love in death

Capulet: Despised, distressed, hated, martyred, killed!
Uncomfortable time, why came you now
To murder, murder our solemnity?
O child! O child! my soul, and not my child!
Dead are you, dead! alack, my child is dead,
And with my child my joys are buried!

Friar Laurence: Peace, ho, for shame! Confusion's cure lives not
In these confusions. Heaven and yourself
Had part in this fair maid! now heaven has all,
And all the better is it for the maid.
Your part in her you could not keep from death,
But heaven keeps his part in eternal life.
The most you sought was her promotion,
For 'twas your heaven she should be advanced;
And weep you now, seeing she is advanced
Above the clouds, as high as heaven itself?
O, in this love, you love your child so ill
That you run mad, seeing that she is well.
She's not well married that lives married long,
But she's best married that dies married young.
Dry up your tears and stick your rosemary
On this fair corpse, and, as the custom is,
In all her best array bear her to church;
For though fond nature bids us all lament,
Yet nature's tears are reason's merriment.

Capulet: All things that we ordained festival
Turn from their office to black funeral—
Our instruments to melancholy bells,
Our wedding cheer to a sad burial feast;
Our solemn hymns to sullen dirges change;
Our bridal flowers serve for a buried corpse;
And all things change them to the contrary.

Friar Laurence: Sir, go you in; and, madam, go with him;
And go, Sir Paris. Every one prepare
To follow this fair corpse unto her grave.
The heavens do lower upon you for some ill;
Move them no more by crossing their high will.

[*Exit except for Musicians and Nurse*]

First Musician: Faith, we may put up our pipes and be gone.

Nurse: Honest good fellows, ah, put up, put up!
For well you know this is a pitiful case.

[*Exit*]

First Musician: Ay, by my troth, the case may be amended.

All things that we ordained festival
Turn from their office to black funeral

[*Enter Peter*]

Peter: Musicians, O, musicians, "Heart's ease," "Heart's ease"!
O, if you will have me live, play "Heart's ease."

First Musician: Why "Heart's ease"?

Peter: O, musicians, because my heart itself plays "My heart is full of woe." O, play me some merry dump to comfort me.

First Musician: Not a dump we! 'Tis no time to play now.

Peter: You will not then?

First Musician: No.

Peter: I will then give it you soundly.

First Musician: What will you give us?

Peter: No money, on my faith, but the gleek. I will give you the minstrel.

First Musician: Then will I give you the serving-creature.

Peter: Then will I lay the serving-creature's dagger on your pate. I will carry no crotchets. I'll re you, I'll fa you. Do you note me?

First Musician: If you re us and fa us, you note us.

Second Musician: Pray you put up your dagger, and put out your wit.

Peter: Then have at you with my wit! I will dry-beat you with an iron wit, and put up my iron dagger. Answer me like men.

When griping grief the heart does wound,
And doleful dumps the mind oppress,
Then music with her silver sound—

Why "silver sound"? Why "music with her silver sound"?
What say you, Simon Catling?

First Musician: Surely, sir, because silver has a sweet sound.

Peter: Pretty! What say you, Hugh Rebeck?

Second Musician: I say "silver sound" because musicians sound for silver.

Peter: Pretty too! What say you, James Soundpost?

Third Musician: Faith, I know not what to say.

Peter: O, I cry you mercy! you are the singer. I will say for you. It is "music with her silver sound" because musicians have no gold for sounding.

Then music with her silver sound
With speedy help does lend redress.

[*Exit*]

First Musician: What a pestilent knave is this same?

Second Musician: Hang him, Jack! Come, we'll in here, tarry for the mourners, and stay dinner.

[*Exit*]

Act Five

1

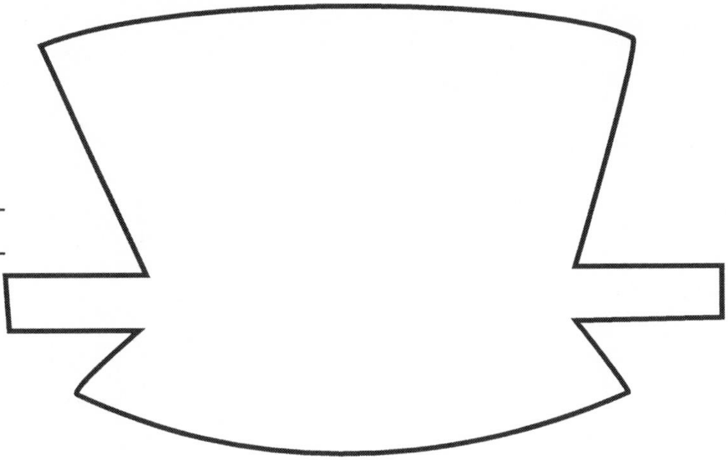

[*Mantua. A street*]

[*Enter Romeo*]

Romeo: If I may trust the flattering truth of sleep
My dreams presage some joyful news at hand.
My bosom's lord sits lightly in his throne,
And all this day an unaccustomed spirit
Lifts me above the ground with cheerful thoughts.
I dreamt my lady came and found me dead
(Strange dream that gives a dead man leave to think!)
And breathed such life with kisses in my lips
That I revived and was an emperor.
Ah me! how sweet is love itself possessed,
When but love's shadows are so rich in joy!

[*Enter Balthasar*]

News from Verona! How now, Balthasar?
Do you not bring me letters from the friar?
How does my lady? Is my father well?
How fares my Juliet? That I ask again,
For nothing can be ill if she be well.

Balthasar: Then she is well, and nothing can be ill.
Her body sleeps in Capel's monument,
And her immortal part with angels lives.
I saw her laid low in her kindred's vault
And presently took post to tell it you.
O, pardon me for bringing these ill news,
Since you did leave it for my office, sir.

Romeo: Is it even so? Then I defy you, stars!
You know my lodging. Get me ink and paper
And hire posthorses. I will go forth tonight.

Balthasar: I do beseech you, sir, have patience.
Your looks are pale and wild and do import
Some misadventure.

Romeo: Tush, you are deceived.
Leave me and do the thing I bid you do.
Have you no letters to me from the friar?

Balthasar: No, my good lord.

Romeo: No matter. Get you gone
And hire those horses. I'll be with you straight.

[*Exit Balthasar*]

How fares my Juliet? That I ask again,
For nothing can be ill if she be well.

Romeo: Well, Juliet, I will lie with you tonight.
Let's see for means. O mischief, you are swift
To enter in the thoughts of desperate men!
I do remember an apothecary,
And hereabouts 'a dwells, which late I noted
In tattered weeds, with overwhelming brows,
Culling of simples. Meager were his looks,
Sharp misery had worn him to the bones;
And in his needy shop a tortoise hung,
An alligator stuffed, and other skins
Of ill-shaped fishes; and about his shelves
A beggarly account of empty boxes,
Green earthen pots, bladders, and musty seeds,
Remnants of packthread, and old cakes of roses
Were thinly scattered, to make up a show.
Noting this penury, to myself I said,
"But if a man did need a poison now
Whose sale is present death in Mantua,
Here lives a caitiff wretch would sell it him."
O, this same thought did but forerun my need,
And this same needy man must sell it me.
As I remember, this should be the house.
Being holiday, the beggar's shop is shut. What, ho!
apothecary!

But if a man did need a poison now

[*Enter Apothecary*]

Apothecary: Who calls so loud?

Romeo: Come here, man. I see that you are poor.
Hold, there is forty ducats. Let me have
A dram of poison, such soon-speeding gear
As will disperse itself through all the veins
That the life-weary taker may fall dead,
And that the trunk may be discharged of breath
As violently as hasty powder fired
Does hurry from the fatal cannon's womb.

Apothecary: Such mortal drugs I have; but Mantua's law
Is death to any he that utters them.

Romeo: Are you so bare and full of wretchedness
And fear to die? Famine is in your cheeks,
Need and oppression starveth in your eyes,
Contempt and beggary hangs upon your back:
The world is not your friend, nor the world's law;
The world affords no law to make you rich;
Then be not poor, but break it and take this.

Apothecary: My poverty but not my will consents.

Romeo: I pay your poverty and not your will.

Apothecary: Put this in any liquid thing you will
And drink it off, and if you had the strength
Of twenty men, it would dispatch you straight.

Romeo: There is your gold— worse poison to men's souls,
Doing more murder in this loathsome world,
Than these poor compounds that you may not sell.
I sell you poison; you have sold me none.
Farewell. Buy food and get yourself in flesh.
Come, cordial and not poison, go with me
To Juliet's grave; for there must I use you.

[*Exit*]

Put this in any liquid thing you will and drink it off

2

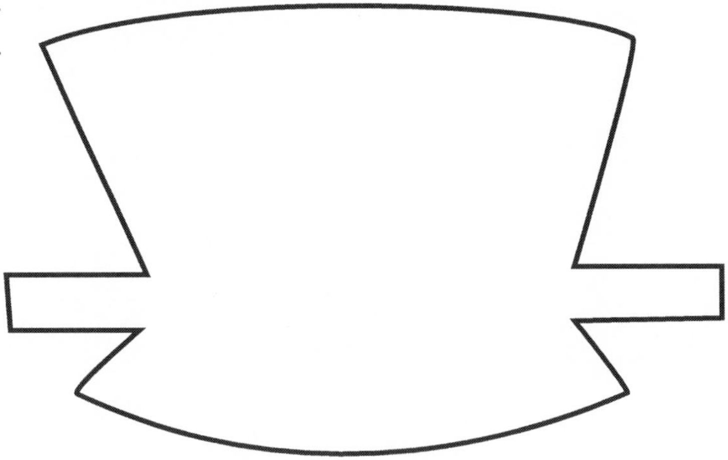

[Verona. Friar Laurence's cell]

[Enter Friar John]

Friar John: Holy Franciscan friar, brother, ho!

[Enter Friar Laurence]

Friar Laurence: This same should be the voice of Friar John.
Welcome from Mantua. What says Romeo?
Or, if his mind be writ, give me his letter.

Friar John: Going to find a barefoot brother out,
One of our order, to associate me
Here in this city visiting the sick,
And finding him, the searchers of the town,
Suspecting that we both were in a house
Where the infectious pestilence did reign,
Sealed up the doors, and would not let us forth,
So that my speed to Mantua there was stayed.

Friar Laurence: Who bare my letter, then, to Romeo?

Friar John: I could not send it— here it is again—
Nor get a messenger to bring it you,
So fearful were they of infection.

Friar Laurence: Unhappy fortune! By my brotherhood,
The letter was not nice, but full of charge,
Of dear import; and the neglecting it
May do much danger. Friar John, go hence,
Get me an iron crow and bring it straight
Unto my cell.

Friar John: Brother, I'll go and bring it you.

[Exit]

Friar Laurence: Now, must I to the monument alone.
Within this three hours will fair Juliet wake.
She will beshrew me much that Romeo
Has had no notice of these accidents;
But I will write again to Mantua,
And keep her at my cell till Romeo come—
Poor living corpse, closed in a dead man's tomb!

[Exit]

What says Romeo?
Or, if his mind be writ, give me his letter.

3

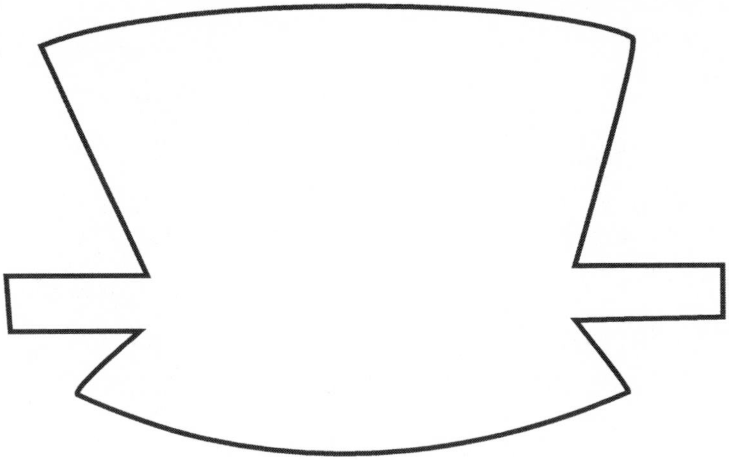

[*Verona churchyard, at the sepoykcger of the Capulets*]

[*Enter Paris and his Page with flowers and a torch*]

Paris: Give me your torch, boy. Go off, and stand aloof.
Yet put it out, for I would not be seen.
Under that yew tree lay you all along,
Holding your ear close to the hollow ground.
So shall no foot upon the churchyard tread
Being loose, unfirm, with digging up of graves
But you shall hear it. Whistle then to me,
As signal that you hear something approach.
Give me those flowers. Do as I bid you, go.

Page: [*aside*] I am almost afraid to stand alone
Here in the churchyard; yet I will adventure.

[*Retires*]

Paris: Sweet flower, with flowers your bridal bed I strew
(O woe! your canopy is dust and stones)
Which with sweet water nightly I will dew;
Or, wanting that, with tears distilled by moans.
The obsequies that I for you will keep
Nightly shall be to strew, your grave and weep.

[*Boy Whistles*]

The boy gives warning something does approach.
What cursed foot wanders this way tonight
To cross my obsequies and true love's rite?
What, with a torch? Muffle me, night, awhile.

[*Retires*]

The boy gives warning something does approach.

[*Enter Romeo, and Balthasar with torch, mattock, crowbar*]

Romeo: Give me that mattock and the wrenching iron.
Hold, take this letter. Early in the morning
See you deliver it to my lord and father.
Give me the light. Upon your life I charge you,
Whatever you hear or see, stand all aloof
And do not interrupt me in my course.
Why I descend into this bed of death
Is partly to behold my lady's face,
But chiefly to take there from her dead finger
A precious ring— a ring that I must use
In dear employment. Therefore, be gone.
But if you, jealous, do return to pry
In what I farther shall intend to do,
By heaven, I will tear you joint by joint
And strew this hungry churchyard with your limbs.
The time and my intents are savage-wild,
More fierce and more inexorable far
Than empty tigers or the roaring sea.

Balthasar: I will be gone, sir, and not trouble you.

Romeo: So shall you show me friendship. Take you that.
Live, and be prosperous; and farewell, good fellow.

Balthasar: [*aside*] For all this same, I'll hide me hereabout.
His looks I fear, and his intents I doubt.

[*Retires*]

Romeo: You detestable maw, you womb of death,
Gorged with the dearest morsel of the earth,
Thus I enforce your rotten jaws to open,
And in despite I'll cram you with more food.

[*Romeo opens the tomb*]

stand all aloof
And do not interrupt me in my course.

Paris: This is that banished haughty Montague
That murdered my love's cousin— with which grief
It is supposed the fair creature died—
And here is come to do some villanous shame
To the dead bodies. I will apprehend him.
Stop your unhallowed toil, vile Montague!
Can vengeance be pursued further than death?
Condemned villain, I do apprehend you.
Obey, and go with me; for you must die.

Romeo: I must indeed; and therefore came I here.
Good gentle youth, tempt not a desperate man.
Fly away and leave me. Think upon these gone;
Let them affright you. I beseech you, youth,
Put not another sin upon my head
By urging me to fury. O, be gone!
By heaven, I love you better than myself,
For I come here armed against myself.
Stay not, be gone. Live, and hereafter say
A madman's mercy bid you run away.

Paris: I do defy your conjuration
And apprehend you for a felon here.

Romeo: Will you provoke me? Then have at you, boy!

[*They fight*]

Page: O Lord, they fight! I will go call the watch.

[*Exit. Paris falls*]

Paris: O, I am slain! If you be merciful,
Open the tomb, lay me with Juliet.

[*Dies*]

Stop your unhallowed toil, vile Montague!

Romeo: In faith, I will. Let me peruse this face.
Mercutio's kinsman, noble Count Paris!
What said my man when my betossed soul
Did not attend him as we rode? I think
He told me Paris should have married Juliet.
Said he not so? or did I dream it so?
Or am I mad, hearing him talk of Juliet
To think it was so? O, give me your hand,
One writ with me in sour misfortune's book!
I'll bury you in a triumphant grave.
A grave? O, no, a lantern, slaughtered youth,
For here lies Juliet, and her beauty makes
This vault a feasting presence full of light.
Death, lie you there, by a dead man interred.

[*Lays him in the tomb*]

How often when men are at the point of death
Have they been merry! which their keepers call
A lightning before death. O, how may I
Call this a lightning? O my love! my wife!
Death, that has sucked the honey of your breath,
Has had no power yet upon your beauty.
You are not conquered. Beauty's ensign yet
Is crimson in your lips and in your cheeks,
And death's pale flag is not advanced there.
Tybalt, lie you there in your bloody sheet?
O, what more favor can I do to you
Than with that hand that cut your youth in twain
To sunder his that was your enemy?
Forgive me, cousin. Ah, dear Juliet,
Why are you yet so fair? Shall I believe
That unsubstantial Death is amorous,
And that the lean abhorred monster keeps
You here in dark to be his paramour?
For fear of that I still will stay with you
And never from this palace of dim night
Depart again. Here, here will I remain
With worms that are your chambermaids. O, here
Will I set up my everlasting rest
And shake the yoke of inauspicious stars
From this world-wearied flesh. Eyes, look your last!
Arms, take your last embrace! and, lips, O you
The doors of breath, seal with a righteous kiss
A dateless bargain to engrossing death!
Come, bitter conduct; come, unsavory guide!
You desperate pilot, now at once run on
The dashing rocks your seasick weary bark!
Here's to my love!

[*Drinks*]

O true apothecary!
Your drugs are quick. Thus with a kiss I die.

[*Falls*]

Death, lie you there, by a dead man interred.

[*Enter Friar Laurence, with lantern, crowbar, and spade*]

Friar Laurence: Saint Francis be my speed! how often tonight
Have my old feet stumbled at graves! Who's there?

Balthasar: Here's one, a friend, and one that knows you well.

Friar Laurence: Bliss be upon you! Tell me, good my friend,
What torch is there that vainly lends his light
To grubs and eyeless skulls? As I discern,
It burns in the Capels' monument.

Balthasar: It does so, holy sir; and there's my master,
One that you love.

Friar Laurence: Who is it?

Balthasar: Romeo.

Friar Laurence: How long has he been there?

Balthasar: Full half an hour.

Friar Laurence: Go with me to the vault.

Balthasar: I dare not, sir.
My master knows not but I am gone hence,
And fearfully did menace me with death
If I did stay to look on his intents.

Friar Laurence: Stay then; I'll go alone. Fear comes upon me.
O, much I fear some ill unthrifty thing.

Balthasar: As I did sleep under this yew tree here,
I dreamt my master and another fought,
And that my master slew him.

Friar Laurence: Romeo!
Alack, alack, what blood is this which stains
The stony entrance of this sepulchre?
What mean these masterless and gory swords
To lie discolored by this place of peace?

[*Enters the tomb*]

Romeo! O, pale! Who else? What, Paris too?
And steeped in blood? Ah, what an unkind hour
Is guilty of this lamentable chance! The lady stirs.

[*Juliet rises*]

Juliet: O comfortable friar! where is my lord?
I do remember well where I should be,
And there I am. Where is my Romeo?

Friar Laurence: I hear some noise. Lady, come from that nest
Of death, contagion, and unnatural sleep.
A greater power than we can contradict
Has thwarted our intents. Come, come away.
Your husband in your bosom there lies dead;
And Paris too. Come, I'll dispose of you
Among a sisterhood of holy nuns.
Stay not to question, for the watch is coming.
Come, go, good Juliet. I dare no longer stay.

Juliet: Go, get you gone, for I will not away.

[*Exit Friar*]

What's here? A cup, closed in my true love's hand?
Poison, I see, has been his timeless end.
O churl! drunk all, and left no friendly drop
To help me after? I will kiss your lips.
Haply some poison yet does hang on them
To make me die with a restorative.

[*Kisses him*]

Your lips are warm!

Chief Watch: [within] Lead, boy. Which way?

Juliet: Yea, noise? Then I'll be brief. O happy dagger!

[*Snatches Romeo's dagger*]

This is your sheath; there rest, and let me die.

[*She stabs herself and falls on top of Romeo*]

A greater power than we can contradict
Has thwarted our intents.

[*Enter Paris's Page and Watchman*]

Page: This is the place. There, where the torch does burn.

Chief Watch: The ground is bloody. Search about the churchyard.
Go, some of you; whoever you find, attach.

[*Exit some of the Watch*]

Pitiful sight! here lies the Count slain;
And Juliet bleeding, warm, and newly dead,
Who here has lain this two days buried.
Go, tell the Prince; run to the Capulets;
Raise up the Montagues; some others search.

[*Exit the rest of the Watch*]

We see the ground whereon these woes do lie,
But the true ground of all these piteous woes
We cannot without circumstance descry.

[*Enter Watchmen with Balthasar*]

Second Watch: Here's Romeo's man. We found him in the churchyard.

Chief Watch: Hold him in safety till the Prince come here.

[*Enter Friar Laurence and a Watchman*]

Third Watch: Here is a friar that trembles, sighs, and weeps.
We took this mattock and this spade from him
As he was coming from this churchyard side.

Chief Watch: A great suspicion! Stay the friar too.

here lies the Count slain;
And Juliet bleeding, warm, and newly dead

[Enter the Prince and his party]

Prince: What misadventure is so early up,
That calls our person from our morning rest?

[Enter Capulet, his Wife, and others]

Capulet: What should it be, that they so shriek abroad?

Lady Capulet: The people in the street cry "Romeo,"
Some "Juliet," and some "Paris"; and all run,
With open outcry, toward our monument.

Prince: What fear is this which startles in our ears?

Chief Watch: Sovereign, here lies the Count Paris slain;
And Romeo dead; and Juliet, dead before,
Warm and new killed.

Prince: Search, seek, and know how this foul murder comes.

Chief Watch: Here is a friar, and slaughtered Romeo's man,
With instruments upon them fit to open
These dead men's tombs.

Capulet: O heavens! O wife, look how our daughter bleeds!
This dagger has mistaken, for, lo, his house
Is empty on the back of Montague,
And it missheathed in my daughter's bosom!

Lady Capulet: O me! this sight of death is as a bell
That warns my old age to a sepulcher.

[Enter Montague and others]

Prince: Come, Montague; for you are early up
To see your son and heir more early down.

Montague: Alas, my liege, my wife is dead tonight!
Grief of my son's exile has stopped her breath.
What further woe conspires against my age?

Prince: Look, and you shall see.

Montague: O you untaught! what manners is in this,
To press before your father to a grave?

Prince: Seal up the mouth of outrage for a while,
Till we can clear these ambiguities
And know their spring, their head, their true descent;
And then will I be general of your woes
And lead you even to death. Meantime forbear,
And let mischance be slave to patience.
Bring forth the parties of suspicion.

The people in the street cry "Romeo,"
Some "Juliet," and some "Paris"

Friar Laurence: I am the greatest, able to do least,
Yet most suspected, as the time and place
Does make against me, of this direful murder;
And here I stand, both to impeach and purge
Myself condemned and myself excused.

Prince: Then say it once what you do know in this.

Friar Laurence: I will be brief, for my short date of breath
Is not so long as is a tedious tale.
Romeo, there dead, was husband to that Juliet;
And she, there dead, that Romeo's faithful wife.
I married them; and their stolen marriage day
Was Tybalt's doomsday, whose untimely death
Banished the new-made bridegroom from this city;
For whom, and not for Tybalt, Juliet pined.
You, to remove that siege of grief from her,
Betrothed and would have married her perforce
To Count Paris. Then comes she to me
And with wild looks bid me devise some mean
To rid her from this second marriage,
Or in my cell there would she kill herself.
Then gave I her (so tutored by my art)
A sleeping potion; which so took effect
As I intended, for it wrought on her
The form of death. Meantime I writ to Romeo
That he should here come as this dire night
To help to take her from her borrowed grave,
Being the time the potion's force should cease.
But he which bore my letter, Friar John,
Was stayed by accident, and yesternight
Returned my letter back. Then all alone
At the prefixed hour of her waking
Came I to take her from her kindred's vault;
Meaning to keep her closely at my cell
Till I conveniently could send to Romeo.
But when I came, some minute before the time
Of her awaking, here untimely lay
The noble Paris and true Romeo dead.
She wakes; and I entreated her come forth
And bear this work of heaven with patience;
But then a noise did scare me from the tomb,
And she, too desperate, would not go with me,
But, as it seems, did violence on herself.
All this I know, and to the marriage
Her nurse is privy; and if aught in this
Miscarried by my fault, let my old life
Be sacrificed, some hour before his time,
Unto the rigor of severest law.

Prince: We still have known you for a holy man.
Where's Romeo's man? What can he say in this?

Romeo, there dead, was husband to that Juliet;
And she, there dead, that Romeo's faithful wife.

Balthasar: I brought my master news of Juliet's death;
And then in post he came from Mantua
To this same place, to this same monument.
This letter he early bid me give his father,
And threatened me with death, going in the vault,
If I departed not and left him there.

Prince: Give me the letter. I will look on it.
Where is the Count's page that raised the watch?
Sirrah, what made your master in this place?

Page: He came with flowers to strew his lady's grave;
And bid me stand aloof, and so I did.
Soon comes one with light to open the tomb;
And by-and-by my master drew on him;
And then I ran away to call the watch.

Prince: This letter does make good the friar's words,
Their course of love, the tidings of her death;
And here he writes that he did buy a poison
Of a poor apothecary, and therewithal
Came to this vault to die, and lie with Juliet.
Where be these enemies? Capulet, Montague,
See what a scourge is laid upon your hate,
That heaven finds means to kill your joys with love!
And I, for winking at you, discords too,
Have lost a brace of kinsmen. All are punished.

Capulet: O brother Montague, give me your hand.
This is my daughter's jointure, for no more
Can I demand.

Montague: But I can give you more;
For I will raise her statue in pure gold,
That while Verona by that name is known,
There shall no figure at such rate be set
As that of true and faithful Juliet.

Capulet: As rich shall Romeo's by his lady's lie—
Poor sacrifices of our enmity!

Prince: A glooming peace this morning with it brings.
The sun for sorrow will not show his head.
Go hence, to have more talk of these sad things;
Some shall be pardoned, and some punished;
For never was a story of more woe
Than this of Juliet and her Romeo.

[*Exit omnes*]

This letter does make good the friar's words,
Their course of love, the tidings of her death

Curtain Call

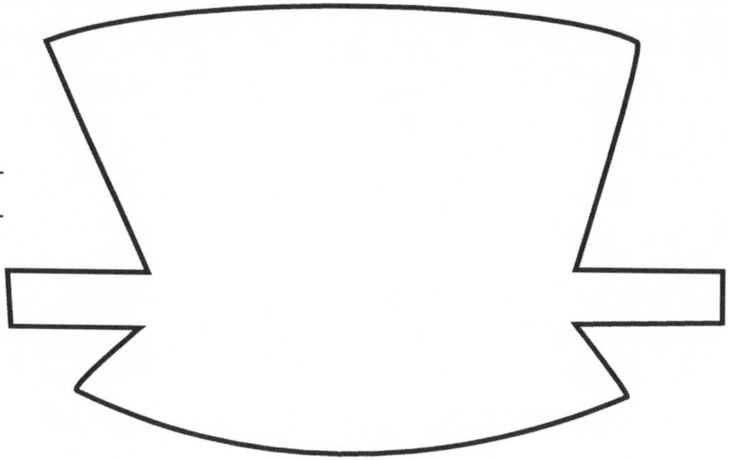

[*Actors take their bows*]

The End

Contents

alderman : elected city official
ambuscado : ambush
amerce : assess a heavy fine or penalty
atomies : tiny creatures
Benedicite : blessing
caitiff : coward, wretch
cankered : ulcerated, corrupted
chapless : with no lower jaw
cheveril : soft leather
choler : anger
cockatrice : serpent born of a cock's egg, which can kill at a glance
collier : coal miner
Cophetua : King Cophetua, a medieval legend
corse : corpse
cot-quean : scolding woman
court-cubbert : sideboard with three tiers; cupboard
crotchet : odd notion, small hook
crowkeeper : scarecrow
Cupid : god of desire and love
cuz : cousin, relative
demesnes : territories, landed estates
Dian : Diana, goddess of the hunt, a celibate goddess
dishclout : dishcloth
dug : nipple
dram : small amount, short drink
dun : grayish brown
elflock : tangled hair
ell : about a cubit, length of a forearm.
endite : write
flirt-gill : loose woman
gleek : joke, scoffing

hilding : wretch

iron crow : crowbar

join-stool : joint stools have braces at the bottom

Lammas Eve : Lammas, celebration of the first wheat harvest

maidenhead : hymen

mammet : or maumet; straw figure

marchpane : marzipan

masque : courtly entertainment of music, dancing, theatrics, singing, costumes

mattock : wide-bladed pickaxe

mewed : confined

mickle : great

orison : prayer

osier : willow

packthread : twine

painted bow : The Tatar composite bow was typically made of horn and decorated.

passado : fencing maneuver

plantain leaf : used medicinally for skin sores or rashes

poor-John : cod-like fish

poperin pear : Flemish fruit with suggestive shape

prorogued : legislature out of session

purblind : partially blind

Queen Mab : fairy who ruled over dreams

rood : crucifix

ropery : roguish or criminal behavior

scathe : injure or harm

shrift : confession

shrived : heard in confession

simples : medicinal plants

skains-mate : messmate

surcease : cessation

swits : switches, flexible branches used for whipping

Tartar : or Tatar, a people also known as the Golden Horde, who dominated Eastern Europe through the 14th and 15th centuries, renowned for their terrorism in conquering other peoples.

thrice : three times

tithe-pig : pig given as a tithe

topgallant : upper sail

visor : half-mask for masquerading

winged messenger : Mercury, or Hermes, with wings on his feet, to carry news from the gods.

wormwood : artemisia, bitter herb

AUTHOR

William Shakespeare, *the third of eight children, was born on April 23, 1564 in the English market town of Stratford-upon-Avon. His father became the mayor of Stratford in 1568 and worked as a glovemaker and a moneylender. Four years after leaving school at approximately the age of fourteen, Shakespeare married Anne Hathaway in November of 1582; their first child Susannah was born in May of the following year. Two years later, Anne gave birth to twins, Hamnet and Judith. Between 1585 and 1592, a period called "the lost years," there is almost no evidence about Shakespeare's life, nor is there any solid evidence about how or why he made his way to London to become a dramatist. By 1592, however, Shakespeare's reputation as a playwright and poet had begun to grow. In 1594, he helped found a new theater company, the Lord Chamberlain's Men, and became the company's dramatist. Shakespeare's success increased, and by 1598, the year he registered* The Merchant of Venice, *he had already purchased one of the biggest residences in Stratford. Some of Shakespeare's richest dramatic work was written after the founding of the Globe Theater by the Lord Chamberlain's Men in 1599, including* Julius Caesar, Hamlet, Othello, King Lear, *and* Macbeth. *After 1611, Shakespeare largely retired from the theater to spend more time in Stratford. He died in 1616 on his birthday, April 23, when he was fifty-two years old.*

EDITOR

Sasha "Birdie" Newborn: Editor of classic texts for 30 years, with a concentration on the Nineteenth Century, based on a wealth of experience in the small press world of printing and book production. Also translator, proofreader, book doctor, and publisher. First publishing was an "underground newspaper" called Middle Earth for one year out of Iowa City, followed by most of a year with Liberation News Service, then five years spent with various New York publishers as a temporary typist, proofreader, indexer — eeventually settling in Santa Barbara as partner in a poetry press, and editing a literary journal. When that collaboration split, Bandanna Books emerged as a vehicle for college classics and writing books. Shakespeare is another mountain to climb, from an editor's desk point of view. If S. were alive, how would he edit these lines? Actually, as far as we know (we don't know), Shakespeare never oversaw any editing or printing of his plays, which were published after his death. As editor, my belief is that he would be incredulous that his work continues to delight new audiences.

Producer

The Producer is the Business Manager; this person is responsible for money matters. That starts with the budget. The Producer must be satisfied that the Budget is realistic, in order for the show to go on.

Some items will be estimates on future earnings, such as ticket sales. If income falls short of expenses, who is the surety that the bills will be paid? If not the Producer, then it must be someone whom the Producer has enlisted.

If the production is intended to be a profit-making venture, then the Budget is more open-ended, to include continuing expenses vs. continuing revenues, until a point is reached at which it becomes no longer economical to continue.

Next is the program, the booklet handed out at the performance, which ought to look good enough as a souvenir of a wonderful evening. The program is also an important sales tool; it presumably will be filled with advertising paid by sponsors, as well as all the relevant data of the performance—cast, with bios and pictures of the major players, the crew, the staff, supporters, anyone who should be given credit for helping the production.

Publicity also falls in the domain of the Producer, which is essentially the same task as creating the program, but honed for direct mail or email to prospective audience members. Big advantage: people have already heard of the author.

Budget

Income

- Sponsors
- Anticipated ticket sales
- Program ads
- Donors
- Institutional support
- Subscriptions
- Other

Expenses

- Sets and Props
- Costumes
- Theater rental
- Talent
- Contract labor
- Equipment rental
- Program design, printing, mailing
- Advertising
- Ushers and Box Office
- Other

Balance

Program

Synopsis of the play

Playwright, history of the play (if available)

Director, previous accomplishments

Staff, likewise

Bios of the leading players, with photos in costume

Credits for the cast,
 and everyone associated with the production

Space to highlight major donors and sponsors

Design and typesetting

Selling ad space

Cover design

Design ads (if necessary)

Printing

Publicity

Press release

mailing list (if available)

email list

parents (if applicable)

school or institution

paid ads

word-of-mouth

announcements (i.e. auditions)

short YouTube video of rehearsal

Box Office, Ushers, Ticket-takers

Pre-Production

Pre-Production has to do with all those physical pieces that have to be acquired or built before performance: sets, costumes, props, equipment, and the theater itself. The Set Designer and Costume Designer operate more or less independently to produce their pieces, on consultation with the Director as to the effect desired in each scene. Often, the Set Designer also handles or creates the props.

Costumes can be a very creative area, depending on in which time period or fantasy setting that the Director chooses to situate the play. Sumptuary laws—laws that prescribed the style of clothing for citizens, depending on class, were in effect in Shakespeare's time, but they were often disregarded.

Checking on the equipment and the theater ordinarily is the responsibility of the Stage Manager.

Props

Set furniture

crowbars

curtains

pickaxes

beards, mustaches

masquerade masks

letter

musical instruments

vial, cup for poison

swords and daggers

balcony

chairs

rope ladder

Set Design

The director's vision of the play ideally connects Shakespeare's themes with modern sensibilities. Your coherent vision must drive the whole production, from costumes and sets to the dramatic actions, perhaps the regional accents, references to recent local events in the news.

Two essentials in this play—the balcony and the sepulcher—may require sturdy construction, as well as coordination with lighting, as when Juliet speaks to Romeo, then turns to speak to Nurse or Lady Capulet, then turns back again. A different challenge for staging comes several times, as when for the party and the final scene, the stage comes to be crowded with characters, yet the focus must be on the actor speaking..

Director's notes on the scenes:

PROLOGUE

ACT ONE

1 *Street in Verona*

2 *Street*

3 *Capulet's house*

4 *Street*

5 *Capulet's house*

PROLOGUE 2

ACT TWO

1 *Lane outside Capulet's orchard*

2 *Capulet's orchard*

3 *Friar Laurence's cell*

4 *Street*

5 *Capulet's orchard*

6 *Friar Laurence's cell*

ACT THREE

1 *Public place*

2 *Capulet's Orchard*

3 *Friar Laurence's cell*

4 *Capulet's house*

5 *Capulet's orchard*

ACT FOUR

1 *Friar Laurence's cell*

2 *Capulet's house*

3 *Juliet's chamber*

4 *Capulet's house*

5 *Juliet's chamber*

ACT FIVE

1 *Mantua, a street*

2 *Verona, Friar Laurence's cell*

3 *Churchyard, Capulet sepulcher*

Costumes

Appropriate for the vision of the play. Different styles for the two quarreling houses, plus the general public?

Romeo (2 outfits?)

Juliet (2-3 outfits?)

Mercutio

Benvolio

Count Paris

Tybalt

Friar Laurence

Capulet

Lady Capulet

Prince Escalus

Nurse

Montague

Lady Montague

Announcer

Balthasar

Page

Seen in one scene only:

Apothecary

Sampson

Gregory

Abram

Capulet cousin

Peter

Officer

Friar John

Groups, crowds or extras:

Musicians

Chief Watch

Several Watchmen

Citizens

Servants

Masqueraders

Guests

Two Fellows

Stage Management

The Stage Manager's domain is primarily the "Wizard of Oz" position: unseen backstage, but in control of the whole stage, as well as lighting and sound. The task is to coordinate all the elements other than the actors, which includes moving sets on and off the stage, prompting actors if they forget their lines, calling for curtain rise and fall, making sure actors are ready when needed.

A Stage Manager needs to be in communication with the lighting and sound person(s), the stage hands, prompters, actors, musicians (or audio).

The prompter stands behind a side curtain, ready to prompt an actor who misses a line. One prompter on each side is even better.

Stage hands move the scenery around between scenes, and usually are not visible to the audience. Cleverly constructed sets are sturdily built on wheels, in such dimensions as will fit backstage. Got a revolving platform? Great, that's handy for changing whole sets.

Will there be documentation of the production? What about pix of the actors in costume for the playbill? Maybe a short publicity video with part of a rehearsal scene for YouTube or locally shown. Who will do it?

Whatever comes up unexpectedly during the play—a set flat falls over, a light burns out—that's the Stage Manager's new task.

Manager

Prompters

Stage Hands

Lighting

Sound

Photography/Video

Other

Scheduling

The Schedule is determined by the Director, but is usually handled by an aide, or the Assistant Director (if there is one).

Everyone is on the schedule—where they should be and when. A few points on the schedule are fixed, such as the performance dates. Everything else is geared toward the first night of performance.

A useful technique is to work backward from First Night, to figure how long it will take to get X ready, which may be decided in a conference of the responsible parties. The producer may require certain firm commitments before moving forward. The set designer, the wardrobe department, the stage manager may need to find enough personnel to handle their duties in a reasonable time frame.

The Director must determine, given the available resources and people, how long is an adequate period of time to make it all jell—not just the actors but the whole company. Ideally, this decision is a joint one, agreeable to all parties, to maximize coordination of efforts.

Here is a possible sequence of activities:

Production Timeline

Determination that the play is economically feasible

Decision to do the play

Gather team

Team leaders estimate time required

Build timeline schedule

Pick tentative dates for performance

Verify theater availability

Recruit volunteers and begin work

2nd or 3rd week — is the schedule still looking good?

Plunge ahead

Firm up performance dates, hire theater

Midpoint evaluation (point of no return)

set the clock on tasks behind schedule

arrange alternate plan

Doublecheck each area

Troubleshooting snags

Invite reviewers

Final runthrough rehearsal

Performance - first night

Following nights—correct rough spots

Wrap party and congratulations